How to Beat the MONEY-GRABBERS: the Essentials of ESTATE PLANNING

Victor P. Whitney

How to Beat the MONEY-GRABBERS: the Essentials of ESTATE PLANNING

Victor P. Whitney

Manufactured in the United States of America

Library of Congress Cataloging in Publication Data

Whitney, Victor P.
How to beat the money-grabbers.

Includes index.
1. Estate planning—United States. 2. Inheritance and transfer tax—United States. 3. Trusts and trustees—United States. I. Title.
KF750.W48 343'.73'053 79-18518
ISBN 0-87000-442-5

CONTENTS

INTRODUCTION

You can't take it with you, so why not do the next best thing and make certain as much as possible stays with the people you love? The purpose of this book is to make you aware of some of the ideas and concepts which can help you avoid the *money-grabbers* whose primary goal is to deplete your estate.

Who are these *money-grabbers?* The one most familiar to you is the Internal Revenue agent. Not only does he syphon off part of your income during your lifetime, but he can confiscate up to 70% of your estate upon your death. The state tax collector follows close behind. In some instances his share of your estate can exceed that taken by the Internal Revenue Service.

Some lawyers can also be classified as *money-grabbers.* These unscrupulous practitioners look upon probate estates as their own private retirement plans. Fortunately the majority of attorneys who specialize in estate planning will do everything in their power to minimize your estate settlement costs.

There are thousands of vulture-like financial scavengers who circle in wait for your loved ones to receive their inheritances. Get-rich-quick investment schemes abound in our entrepreneurial society and there are purveyors of these schemes on almost every corner.

Another dangerous breed of *money-grabber* is the well-meaning friend who gives financial advice based on half-truths. There is at least one at every cocktail party, and the advice they give, if followed, can be disastrous to your estate.

This book will make you aware of the many ways in which the *money-grabbers* erode your estate. It will take you through the steps involved in analyzing an estate, discuss the advantages and disadvantages of various forms of property transfers, and illustrate many of the vehicles available for use in implementing an estate plan. Such important topics as how to select an executor, guardian, or trustee and what is involved in the probate process are also discussed.

I have discussed estate planning with thousands of people over the past twenty years. Many of them have asked if I could recommend a book that would cover all of the things we talked about. Unfortunately, those books with which I was familiar were either too technical or they did not address the specific types of questions I was being asked. The format and style of this book are designed to be responsive to *your* questions. Hopefully it will be used as a *financial primer* for you and your family and will guide you to a better understanding of estate planning.

This book will not enable you to plan your own estate, but it will give you the background and insight necessary to recognize what steps need to be taken to *BEAT THE MONEY-GRABBERS.*

PART I

ESTATE PLANNING IN GENERAL

CHAPTER I

STEPS IN THE ESTATE PLANNING PROCESS

The more extensive a man's knowledge of what has been done, the greater will be his power of knowing what to do—Disraeli

This chapter provides an overview of the estate planning process. Its purpose is to apprise you of the steps your advisors will follow in planning your estate.

There are six basic elements in the estate planning process:

I. Development of Pertinent Facts.
II. Identification of Problems in Your Existing Plan.
III. Formulation of a Tentative Plan Consistent with Your Present Situation.
IV. Testing Your Estate Plan.
V. Implementing the Plan.
VI. Periodic Review of Your Plan.

I. *DEVELOPMENT OF PERTINENT FACTS*

Before an architect can design your dream home he must determine what style of house you like, what fixtures you want in it, and how much money you can afford to spend. Once he determines what you are looking for in a home and the amount of money you can afford to invest, he will create a design which comes as close to your dream home as your pocketbook will allow. No architect can match your dream to your pocketbook without first obtaining a considerable amount of background information. No estate planner can design a plan to accomplish your objectives without knowing a lot about you, your family, your assets, and your objectives. One of two things will happen if you fail to provide the information your planner needs: either the plan will not accomplish your objectives, or you will end up spending much more time and money than is necessary for changes in the plan which could have been avoided.

Objectives—The single most important element in the fact-finding process is the determination of objectives, but it is also the most difficult. While most people have a general knowledge of what they want to accomplish, they have never taken the time to define those objectives specifically or to determine an order of priority. Think about what it is you want to accomplish for your family. Write down the objectives you feel are important and arrange in order of priority. The following list of possible objectives may or may not pertain to your situation; however, they should stimulate your thinking:

Minimization of Taxes and Other Estate Settlement Costs—Almost everyone is interested in reducing estate settlement costs; however, the importance in relation to other objectives will differ from one person to the next. You need to determine whether cost reduction should have top priority or be secondary to your other objectives.

Simplification in Settling Your Estate—There are several probate avoidance techniques that could shorten and/

or simplify the settlement of your estate; however, there are certain disadvantages incident to each. Those disadvantages may cause you to give simplification a low priority.

Protection for Your Spouse and/or Children—When a person dies, the heirs have no shortage of "financial advisors." Well-meaning friends and relatives as well as a multitude of "financial scavengers" appear on the scene to help manage the money. It is difficult for a widow to say "no" to her brother or her children. Quite often, we read about widows and widowers who have been fleeced by slick-talking strangers who showed them attention when they were emotionally upset. Regardless of how sound our judgment normally is, we do not always act rationally during periods of emotional stress; consequently, it may be desirable to take action to protect the beneficiaries.

Management for Your Spouse and Children—Most people give very little consideration to how their assets will be managed after their deaths. *Who will manage your assets after you are gone?* If your estate is left outright to your spouse or children, they will have to assume the investment responsibilities. But are they capable of keeping the assets productive? Would you be willing to turn full control over to them today? If not, they probably should not have that responsibility after your death.

Income for Your Spouse and Children—It is not a question of whether you want income for them but rather how much income they will need. In deciding how much, you may want to consider the impact of inflation on their income needs.

Education of the Children or Grandchildren—Some people want to enable their children to attend the most expensive private colleges in the country. Others assume their children can work their way through school. Still others would like one or more of their children to study abroad. What kind of education do you want your children or grandchildren to have? Have you given consideration to artistic talents as well as academic abilities? What do you anticipate the costs of their education will be?

Time and Method of Distribution to Minors—Outright distributions to minors will be held and managed by their guardians until they attain majority. In many states, a minor becomes an adult at age eighteen. Most people believe this is too early an age to receive any substantial amount of money. Would you prefer to have distributions withheld until they attain a more mature age? At what age do you think they will have financial maturity? Does the concept of staggered distributions, e.g., one-third at twenty-five, one-third at thirty, and the balance at thirty-five have any appeal to you? Maybe some of your heirs should receive income only and never get distribution of principal, or perhaps each should be treated somewhat differently.

Provision for Other Dependent Relatives—Many people help support their parents or handicapped relatives. If you are providing such support, do you want it to continue in the event of your death?

Providing for a Charity—Quite often people want their assets to benefit some type of charitable organization. Gifts to schools, health causes, and social service groups are common. Some people make outright gifts with no strings attached. Others stipulate their funds be used for a specific purpose. Still others provide income only to the charity so that principal will not be used for the charity's current operating expenses. There are many approaches to charitable gifts.

Continuation, Termination, or Sale of Your Business—Some business owners want their families to continue their businesses. Others would prefer to have their businesses sold as going concerns, and some believe the family would benefit most from a liquidation. The delays involved in making this decision after death could result in substantial losses to the family. The business owner knows his business better than anyone else; consequently, he should make this decision in advance and not leave it up to his executor or the family to decide. The executor may not have all the facts and the family may not be in a sound-enough emotional state to make a rational decision.

The foregoing categories of objectives should provide you with a starting point. As you read through the book, you may identify other objectives which are important to you.

II. *IDENTIFICATION OF PROBLEM AREAS*

When the estate planner has had an opportunity to review your assets, documents, family situation, and objectives, he will be in a position to identify the problems that tend to dilute your estate. The following list of possible problem areas is in no way complete, but it will give you an idea of the kinds of things your advisors will be looking for.

Excessive Estate Settlement Costs—Your existing plan may subject your estate to a great deal of unnecessary costs. Your will or trust, for example, may not take advantage of some of the techniques for reducing estate taxation. Your plan of distribution or the way in which property is titled may cause your estate to pay more than necessary in fees to your executor and attorney.

Possible Unnecessary Delays—The lack of a properly drawn will, improper planning concerning your business, and lack of liquidity are just a few of the things that can delay administration of your estate. A proper estate plan can expedite the handling of your estate.

Unpaid Taxes—Many people postpone paying taxes as long as possible during their lifetimes, but all taxes must be paid before the estate can be settled. Taxes, interest, and penalties increase the liquidity need in your estate. Your executor must pay taxes as quickly as possible to protect your estate from further erosion due to penalties and/or interest.

Last Illness and Funeral Expenses—Many people provide for their funeral and interment in advance; however, it is difficult for them to anticipate the full cost of their last illness. Your planner will attempt to calculate the approximate potential cost. This cost can be increased if proper instructions are not available for your executor. Many people incorporate burial instructions in their wills. Unfortunately, the will may not even be located until after death occurs. Separate instructions left with a family member, your doctor, and your attorney can alleviate this problem.

Inadequacy of Investment Assets to Produce the Income Your Family Needs—After payment of taxes and probate costs, the remaining assets may be insufficient to provide properly for the family. A lot of people have substantial net worths consisting of illiquid non-income-producing assets such as raw land, limited partnerships, and closely held stock. It may be impossible to convert these types of assets into income-producing assets without taking substantial losses.

Lack of Adequate Liquidity—Lack of liquidity is the most serious problem faced in estate settlement. Most estate owners are either inadequately insured or lack other liquid assets sufficient to meet their estate settlement costs. In those instances where there is adequate insurance, the proceeds are often paid to beneficiaries who are unwilling to make them available to the executor for payment of taxes and other costs. This can result in the forced sale of estate assets at a time when the market for those assets is depressed.

Business Continuity—If you have not provided for a buyer or successor management, it is unclear how your business can continue. If you have provided for successor management, your family might still have difficulty obtaining adequate income from the business. Many businesses provide their owners with comfortable livings during their lifetimes; however, when the owner passes away, much of the income formerly enjoyed by the family goes to pay for management assistance.

Problems Related to Guardian, Executor, or Trustee—The person whom you have nominated to serve as executor or trustee may be entirely unqualified to assume such responsibilities, or perhaps you have moved and it would be impossible or impractical for him to act, or maybe he will predecease you or become ill. This type of problem needs to be addressed by the planner and provided for.

Improper Property Titling—The manner in which your assets are titled must tie in with your estate plan. In some instances, assets are held as joint tenants when they should be either in tenants in common or in the contributing tenant's name. In other situations, property should be transferred into joint tenancy. In still others, it might be advisable to hold title in a trust. Improper titling can defeat your entire plan. One of the most common situations planners see is that in which a will has been drawn, which provides exactly the distribution desired, but is completely ineffective since all assets are held in joint tenancy and will pass outright to the surviving joint tenant.

Lack of Business Acumen of the Spouse and/or Children—It is important for the planner to know the extent of each party's business abilities in order to determine whether that person can either manage assets independently or in tandem with a professional trustee. One of the serious deficiencies of estate planning is the fact that most wives are not prepared to face the financial decisions required of them when their husbands pass away. A widow always has some duties to perform and some financial decisions to make. The extent of those responsibilities can be reduced if there is a professional executor or trustee in the picture, but never eliminated. Most widows have had little or no experience in handling business or legal matters. Their lack of awareness of probate and death tax problems makes it difficult for them to recognize when they might need professional assistance or to whom they might turn. And these responsibilities are thrust upon them when their emotional state makes it difficult for them to act rationally. A basic part of any estate plan is to assure that a surviving spouse who has the ability and desire to handle the estate knows how to cope with the realities of the situation.

Family Friction—It is important for the planner to know if any friction exists among family members. If so, great care needs to be taken to avoid placing any of them in a sensitive or controversial position. Many people name one of their children as executor. This often causes conflict where none previously existed because the other children feel the one named as executor is getting more than they are or showing preference to himself in distributing personal effects.

Well-to-Do Beneficiaries—From time to time children become financially successful in their own right or marry into wealthy families. Their income and estate tax situations might make it undesirable to distribute assets outright to them from your estate. The planner should be aware of these situations so that he can develop alternative approaches which minimize taxes, while protecting the children from possible future adversity.

> **Example:** Mr. Gottrocks has an estate of $500,000. He has two children, Golda and Gomer. Golda is a successful physician netting $70,000 per year from her practice and building a substantial estate. She has three children. Gomer works for the telephone company and earns $20,000 per year. He has accumulated very little other than his house and car.
>
> Gomer's share of the estate could be distributed outright to him with no adverse tax consequences; but if Golda were given her share outright, the tax impact would be disastrous both in the income and

estate tax areas. Income earned by the assets would be taxed at the top rate and the assets themselves would be taxed at a high rate in her estate.

One answer might be to leave Golda's share in trust, giving the trustee discretion to distribute income to Golda or her children or to accumulate it. This would spread the income among several beneficiaries in lower tax brackets, but make the income available to Golda should she experience financial reverses. The assets themselves could be distributed to her children upon her death without being totally included in her estate.

The foregoing problems should give you an idea of what your advisors will be looking for when they analyze your existing plan. It is important to know what the specific problem areas are before formulating a tentative plan.

III. *FORMULATING A TENTATIVE PLAN*

Once the problems have been identified, your advisors can address themselves to solving those problems. In some instances, the solution may be as simple as drafting a new will, while in others sophisticated planning tools like private annuities or irrevocable trusts (discussed in later chapters) might come into play.

Each problem should probably be considered independent of all other problems and an ideal solution arrived at for each problem. An ideal solution for one problem may create new problems in another area or be inconsistent with one of your objectives. If this happens, it may be necessary to review priorities or develop a compromise solution.

As you will see, there are many alternatives available to a knowledgeable planner. Ultimately a plan will be arrived at which will accomplish your objectives.

IV. *TESTING THE PLAN*

When a tentative plan has been designed, it must be subjected to an empirical testing process. Your advisors will run a hypothetical administration of the estate to determine taxes and other liquidity needs. They will compare the plan of distribution to your stated objectives and, if it is consistent, present the plan to you. Before you agree to implement the plan, you should fully understand each recommendation. There may be some suggestions that will complicate your life or require a change in your lifestyle. If so, you must either make a commitment to accept the change or ask for alternatives. The only factor in the plan beyond the control of your advisors is your desire to make it work.

V. *IMPLEMENTING THE PLAN*

Once you have agreed to the proposed plan, each member of the estate planning team proceeds to carry out his particular responsibilities.

Your attorney will prepare all of the necessary documents and help you make whatever changes are required in your property titling. The insurance agent will apply for whatever new coverage your family needs and make the necessary changes in your existing insurance.

Your CPA will make whatever revisions he believes are desirable in your accounting system. He will determine fiscal tax years for new entities, ascertain asset values, prepare gift tax returns, and help determine the timing of future asset changes.

A trust officer, while extremely valuable in helping to design the plan, may not be involved immediately in its implementation. If his is a passive role, he will merely review the documents with the attorney to assure his ability to serve. If the plan calls for a living trust, or if investment management services are involved, he will review the investment portfolio with you and indicate the types of changes he believes will best accomplish your objectives.

In many instances, the only member of the estate planning team you will be involved with is your attorney. He is the *only indispensable* team member because he is the only one authorized to practice law. The other advisor who will be involved in most estate plans for younger and middle-aged people is the life insurance man. He is the only team member who can generate instant cash to meet your estate planning objectives.

Whatever plan of action you and your advisors agree upon should be implemented in its entirety if it is going to accomplish your objectives. A plan incomplete is destined to defeat.

VI. *PERIODIC REVIEW*

Once a plan has been implemented, most people want to forget about it, but it cannot be forgotten. Many changes take place either in the law or our personal lives which can have severe impact on what we want to accomplish; consequently, your plan needs to be reviewed periodically. You should initiate that review if changes occur in your situation. Births or deaths of family members, marriage or divorce, significant increases or decreases in assets, or changes in your attitude are some of the occasions for review. Your attorney, or one of the other team members, should initiate the review when there is a change in the law affecting your plan. Such reviews, if timely, will not require the same depth of analysis as your initial estate plan.

CONCLUSION

The estate planning process as discussed in this chapter may appear to be extremely detailed and time consuming; however, once you have assimilated all of the data necessary for your advisors to make their analysis, the majority of estate plans can be designed quickly and simply.

CHAPTER II

JOINT TENANCY AND OTHER PROPERTY INTERESTS

Can one desire too much of a good thing?—Shakespeare

Ownership rights in property can be distinguished in many ways. This chapter will identify various types of property, explain the difference between the source of property and the way in which title is held, and define terms related to ownership. Its purpose is to create an awareness of some of the property concepts with which your attorney works in planning your estate.

TYPES OF PROPERTY

There are three basic types of property: real property, tangible personal property, and intangible personal property. Real property is generally considered to be land, buildings, and all appurtenances. Tangible personal property includes all assets other than real property which can be touched, seen, or felt. Examples of tangible personal property are automobiles, books, furniture, jewelry, and so forth. Intangible personal property is property which represents value, but has no value in and of itself. A stock certificate, for example, is intangible personal property. It represents an interest in a corporation which has value; however, if the certificate is inadvertently destroyed, no value is lost. The certificate can be replaced.

LEGAL OR NOMINAL OWNERSHIP VS. EQUITABLE OR ACTUAL OWNERSHIP

One very important concept for the student of estate planning to understand is that an asset might be in one individual's name (nominal ownership) and yet some or all of the benefits of that asset belong to another (equitable or actual ownership). A trust is an excellent example of this concept. The trustee is the nominal owner and the beneficiary of that trust is the equitable owner. The property is in the trustee's name, but any income or appreciation resulting from the trustee's management will be enjoyed by the beneficiaries.

SOURCE VS. TITLE

There are several ways to take title to property, but there are only two basic sources: separate property and community property. Essentially community property is any property acquired in a community property state by either spouse during marriage other than by gift or inheritance. Separate property is all other property.

COMMUNITY PROPERTY

The eight states with community property laws are Arizona, California, Idaho, Louisiana, New Mexico, Nevada, Texas, and Washington.

In community property states each spouse is deemed to own an undivided one-half interest in such property. Either spouse has a right to dispose of his or her interest in the community by will. If there is no will, the community property normally goes to the surviving spouse under the laws of intestacy.

Community property and joint tenancy are *not* synonymous; however, many residents of community property states often get them confused. Community property, as mentioned earlier, refers to the source of property. It can be titled as community property or it can be held in either spouse's name. If it is titled in joint tenancy, it may lose its status as community property. Some attorneys suggest their clients execute a separate agreement defining the nature of their property. A typical agreement will provide something to this effect: "All of our property, regardless of how it is titled, is community property."

Some non-community property states now recognize community property; and if such interests are properly documented, that property can continue to maintain its community nature in those states. California and perhaps some of the other community property states recognize a hybrid source called quasi-community property for tax purposes. Quasi-community property is property acquired in a non-community property state which would have been community if it had been acquired in California.

FORMS OF HOLDING TITLE

There are five basic ways to hold title to property: One name, joint tenancy, tenancy by the entirety, tenants in common, and community property.

One Name—Any property held by an individual in his name alone in a non-community property state is presumed to be his separate property. When property is held in one name, the owner may sell or otherwise dispose of that property at any time. He also has an absolute right to dispose of it by will upon his death.

Joint Tenancy with Right of Survivorship—Joint tenancy is the most widely used and least understood form of property ownership. Joint tenancy is an arrangement in which two or more people take title to property together. The parties *do not* have to be related. The primary characteristic of joint tenancy is that the surviving joint tenant will receive the entire property regardless of what the deceased joint tenant's will might provide. Why is joint tenancy so commonly used? Some married couples may be emotionally motivated to show their affection and trust by having their assets in both names. Many people use joint tenancy to avoid the costs and delays of probate. Most do it because someone has told them "Everybody takes title as joint tenants." None of these reasons, in and of themselves, should dictate how you take title. No decision concerning how to take title should be made without first discussing the matter with your attorney.

In order to understand some of the problems, let's explore the advantages and disadvantages of joint tenancy.

ADVANTAGES OF JOINT TENANCY:

Avoidance of Probate—The surviving joint tenant or tenants normally succeeds to the deceased joint tenant's interest in the property automatically without having to go through the probate process. This does not necessarily mean there will be cost savings. There may be attorneys' fees and other costs relating specifically to clearing title, preparing tax returns, and so forth. Many attorneys charge up to 1% of the value of joint tenancy assets for clearing title. While costs may or may not be significantly reduced, it is likely that some of the delays of estate administration will be avoided. Property will pass to a surviving joint tenant more quickly than if it passes to the survivor through probate.

Maintains Privacy—Probate records in most states are open to inspection by the public; consequently it is difficult to keep probate matters confidential. Joint tenancy property, on the other hand, will normally pass to the surviving joint tenant without publicity.

Convenience—It is much more convenient to have bank accounts in joint name. Either tenant can withdraw funds if emergencies arise.

Protection from Creditors—In some states, joint tenancy property cannot be reached by creditors of the deceased joint tenant. Any assets in the probate estate would be subject to their claims.

Reduction of State Inheritance Taxes—In some states, inheritance taxes are less on joint tenancy property passing to a surviving spouse than on separately owned property passing to that spouse.

Savings in State Income Taxes—Creation of a joint tenancy in income-producing assets can enable husbands and wives to file separate state income tax returns possibly resulting in some tax savings. Of course, the same result could be achieved through ownership as tenants in common.

DISADVANTAGES OF JOINT TENANCY:

Property Cannot be Disposed of in Accordance with Your Will—A person's will has no effect on joint tenancy property. Many elderly individuals place assets in joint tenancy with one of their children for convenience and in their wills provide for equal distribution among all the children. The child who is a joint tenant receives all of the joint tenancy assets and the other children are effectively disinherited. The answer we often hear when this problem is identified is "My daughter (or son) is a good girl and will divide it among her brothers and sisters." This may be true, but in states which impose inheritance taxes, the taxes will usually be greater than if the property were distributed equally by will.

Taxes May Be Increased If the Non-Contributing Joint Tenant Dies First—A places assets in joint tenancy with B. B dies. A, in effect, inherits his own property back from B. While the surviving joint tenant may be able to prove he contributed the entire consideration for the joint tenancy and thus avoid federal estate taxes, he may end up paying state death taxes on his own property.

Property May Ultimately Pass to Someone You Would Prefer Not to Receive It—A childless couple, for example, has all of their assets in joint tenancy. When the husband dies, his wife, being the survivor, receives all of the joint tenancy property. Upon the wife's subsequent death everything goes to her side of the family if she dies without a will. In effect, joint tenancy in this situation can disinherit one spouse's family. Who gets disinherited depends on which spouse dies first. In the case of a couple with children, there is a possibility the children could be unintentionally disinherited. If a surviving spouse remarries, the new spouse may inherit part or all of the property.

Possible Management Problems—One of the joint tenants normally makes all of the investment decisions relating to the assets. If he dies, the survivor, who has never had to manage the property before, is suddenly burdened with that responsibility. In some cases, this is a desirable result; in others, it could be disastrous.

A Gift Tax May Be Incurred Upon Creation of the Joint Tenancy—Transfer of a bank account into joint tenancy will not be treated as a taxable gift until the noncontributing joint tenant withdraws funds; however, securities placed in joint tenancy will result in an immediate gift equivalent to one-half their value. Creation of joint tenancies in real property are also treated as gifts except that joint tenancy in real property between husband and wife will only be treated as gifts if the donor spouse elects to have it so treated.

Increased Estate Taxes Due to Overqualification for the Marital Deduction—There is an estate deduction allowed for property passing to a surviving spouse. This deduction is limited to the greater of $250,000 or one-half of your adjusted gross estate. When more property passes to a surviving spouse than is necessary to obtain the maximum marital deduction, the estate is considered to be "overqualified." In a $100,000 estate, there will probably be no adverse tax consequences due to overqualification from using joint tenancy. If the estate is $500,000, overqualification may cost the heirs up to $76,500 in unnecessary estate taxes. The puzzle of joint tenancy is one of the most perplexing faced by estate planners. The solution will differ in every case. Some of you should have your assets in joint tenancy and others should not. You may be tempted to switch out of joint tenancy after reading the disadvantages or into it because of the advantages. Please do not do so without consulting your attorney. It is entirely possible transfers in or out of joint tenancy will result in unnecessary gift taxes.

Tenancy By the Entirety—In some states, a husband and wife can hold title to property as tenants by the entirety. This form of ownership is similar to joint tenancy in that the surviving spouse will assume full ownership upon the death of the first spouse. The basic difference between tenancy by the entirety and joint tenancy is that the former cannot be terminated unless both tenants agree, whereas the latter can be terminated by either tenant.

Tenancy in Common—Each tenant in a tenancy in common owns an undivided interest in the property. An example of tenants in common would be "A, B, and C as tenants in common—A as to an undivided one-half interest and B and C each as to an undivided one-quarter interest." If no percentage interest is specified, the tenants are presumed to own the property equally. There is no right of survivorship. A deceased tenant has the right to dispose of his interest in the property under his will; consequently A, in our example, could leave his one-half interest to anyone he chooses.

Community Property—As I mentioned earlier, property acquired from a community property source can be titled as community property. Either spouse can dispose of his or her interest in the community by will. There is no automatic right of survivorship; however, in most community property states, the property will pass to the surviving spouse when there is no will.

OTHER MISCELLANEOUS PROPERTY INTERESTS

Dower and Curtesy—Dower is the right of a widow in the property of her deceased husband and curtesy is the right of a widower in the property of his deceased wife. The laws of each state must be reviewed to determine if, and to what extent, these concepts are still in effect. A typical dower or curtesy interest would entitle the survivor to one-third of the decedent's real property.

Life Estate—A life estate in land is a somewhat self-explanatory property interest. Mrs. Charity B. Quest, who owns Tummy Acres, gives her sister Faith the right to live on and use that property for her lifetime with Tummy Acres going to the American Cancer Society upon Faith's death. In many states, Faith, the life tenant, would have the right to sell Tummy Acres and reinvest the proceeds in other property; however, the proceeds of sale, upon her death, would have to go to the Cancer Society. As a result, life estates can be difficult to police. Also, there might be some adverse tax consequences attributable to life estates. There are some instances where legal life estates can be used; however, in most cases alternative methods of distribution will be preferable.

Leaseholds—From time to time, a landowner will transfer a leasehold interest to a tenant. The tenant agrees to pay rent for a number of years during which time he can construct buildings and divert the property to whatever use he desires. Obviously, a fifty-year land lease relating to property upon which the lessee has constructed income-producing buildings is a valuable asset in the lessee's estate.

Powers of Appointment—A power of appointment is a right to dispose or alter disposition of property being held by a third party. For example, A creates a trust with B as trustee providing for income to C for life, but allowing C to dispose of any remainder by exercising a power of appointment under his will. A is known as the donor of the power and C as holder of the power. There are two basic types of powers of appointment; general powers and special powers. A general power of appointment is one in which the holder of the power has the right to pass his interest in the property on to anyone including his estate or his creditors. The general power can be designed to allow the holder to appoint the property to himself during his lifetime. A special or limited power of appointment is one in which the holder can appoint his interest in the property only to specified individuals or classes of individuals. An example of this type of power is one in which the holder can appoint the property in equal or unequal shares to one or more of his children.

When to Use Powers of Appointment—You may decide to create a trust for the benefit of your spouse either to obtain certain tax advantages or to provide management and protection during your spouse's lifetime. It is your desire that your spouse receive all the income, but upon his or her death, principal is to go to your three children. You can either provide specifically that a certain amount will go to each child or you can give your spouse a power of appointment to determine the share each child will receive. The latter approach provides flexibility to meet the children's changing needs. If one becomes an invalid, and is unable to work, his share might be increased. If another becomes an alcoholic or spendthrift, his share can be decreased. A word of caution. While a power of appointment provides great flexibility it can also become a horrible weapon in the wrong hands. The holder of the power may have a preference for one beneficiary over another or he might be unduly influenced by one of the beneficiaries to exercise the power in his behalf. One of my elderly trust beneficiaries who held such a power would periodically exercise it in favor of one child or another depending on who was paying her the most attention. She ignored the fact that two of the children lived across town while the other three had to travel hundreds of miles to visit her. When granting a power of appointment make certain you understand the donee's emotional makeup.

CONCLUSION

This chapter has provided you with a basic understanding of the various types of ownership interests, methods of holding title, and the distinction between community and separate property. Make certain you provide your advisors with complete and accurate information concerning the source and title of every asset you own. They cannot help you design a workable plan without this information.

CHAPTER III

SETTLING YOUR ESTATE

Let's choose executors and talk of wills—Shakespeare

As you can see from the quotation, the concept of probate has been with us for hundreds of years. The process of probate itself varies from state to state, as do laws relating to wills and intestacy, but every state has some form of probate procedure. This chapter will define some of the terminology related to probate administration and explain the steps in the probate process.

EXECUTOR VS. ADMINISTRATOR

When you pass away your estate will be settled by either an executor or administrator. The executor is the person named in your will to administer your estate. An administrator is a person who is authorized to administer your estate if you do not have a will or the person named in the will cannot or will not act. A woman handling the estate would be called executrix or administratrix. The term "personal representative" is used in most states to refer to both executors and administrators and in some states is the only official designation given to the person who handles the estate.

WHO CAN SERVE?

If you nominate a personal representative in your will, that person will normally be appointed if he qualifies. It is always desirable to name an alternate in case your primary nominee is unable or unwilling to serve or fails to qualify for some other reason. Individuals die, become ill, move from state to state (some states require the executor to be a resident), or are prone to travel extensively. They may be unavailable when needed; consequently, you should consider naming a bank or trust company either as primary or alternate personal representative.

If you do not nominate a personal representative, the probate court will determine who is entitled to appointment. The order of priority of persons who can serve may vary somewhat from state to state; however a typical order of priority might be as follows:

1. Surviving spouse
2. Adult children
3. Adult grandchildren
4. Parents
5. Siblings
6. Aunts and uncles
7. Cousins, etc.
8. Creditors
9. Public administrator

Any person entitled to appointment may renounce in favor of another in order of priority or request that a bank or trust company be appointed. When there is conflict among several individuals of the same priority, the court will often appoint a corporate fiduciary to serve instead of any of the individuals.

PERSONAL REPRESENTATIVE'S BOND

In most states personal representatives are required to be bonded in order to protect heirs from such things as misappropriation of funds, theft, and so forth. The amount of bond will vary from state to state but is usually equivalent to twice the value of personal property in the estate.

Banks and trust companies are normally not required to be bonded; however, the entire assets of those institutions stand behind their administration. In some states, you can relieve your personal representative of the necessity for being bonded. This may be desirable if the personal representative is the sole beneficiary; however, careful consideration should be given to requiring bond if someone other than a sole beneficiary is named. If the personal representative is not bonded, there is virtually no protection for the beneficiaries should he divert estate assets to his own benefit. The cost of a personal representative's bond may vary from state to state but it usually averages about $3 per thousand of personal property value under $100,000 and $2 per thousand over $100,000.

PERSONAL REPRESENTATIVE'S DUTIES

The duties of a personal representative can be divided into eight categories: assembling the assets, protecting the assets, valuation, managing the assets during probate, paying creditors, determining and paying taxes, accounting, and distributing assets.

Assembling the Assets—The personal representative must locate all assets belonging to the decedent.

Bank Accounts—A diligent search should be performed for any bankbooks or other evidence of bank accounts in the decedent's home. If there is any indication undiscovered bank accounts might exist, the personal representative should contact every bank and savings and loan in the community to determine whether or not such accounts do, in fact, exist.

Safe Deposit Box—The safe deposit box may contain evidence of various assets. In most states the box may not be opened except to withdraw a decedent's will unless a representative of the state tax authority is present. The official box opening can normally be arranged within a few weeks after the date of death. If the box contains items such as rings, coins, or other assets with somebody else's name on them, they should not automatically be turned over to that person. Sometimes people label assets as belonging to someone else in order to avoid taxation. Inasmuch as the tax authorities will have records of these items when the box is opened, the personal representative should not relinquish possession until the assumed owner provides proof of ownership. As with the bank accounts, the decedent may have more than one safe deposit box; consequently it may be necessary to inquire among other financial institutions as to the existence of additional boxes.

Personal Effects—The personal representative should immediately inventory all of the decedent's furniture and personal effects. Items appearing to have significant value should be moved to a safe place. If there is a surviving spouse who inherits personal effects, those items can usually be released to the surviving spouse as soon as they have been inventoried and valued.

Brokerage Accounts—Brokerage accounts must be closed immediately. If the account is not closed in timely fashion, the personal representative may be held personally liable for any losses the estate might incur. The existence of brokerage accounts is usually ascertained when statements are found among the decedent's effects.

Other Assets—Deeds for real property, stock certificates, limited partnership interests, and so forth will usually be either among the decedent's personal effects or in his safe deposit box.

Protecting the Assets—The personal representative's second duty is to safeguard the decedent's assets. All valuable items—jewelry, works of art, bearer securities, and so forth—should be stored in a safe place. Unoccupied real property should be secured in the best way possible. For example, it might be desirable to hire a "housesitter" for a residence or a watchman to keep an eye on business properties. Perishables, such as crops, must be disposed of before they spoil if at all possible. Debts owed to the decedent must be collected. Real property must be adequately insured or the personal representative will be held personally liable. He also needs to ascertain whether or not property taxes are up to date. If not, they should be paid to protect the property.

Valuation of Assets—In some states the personal representative makes his own appraisals and in others the court appoints an appraiser. The personal representative uses these values for tax purposes; consequently they should be as accurate as possible because they are subject to close scrutiny by the taxing authorities. Values for listed securities are readily available; however, real property—jewelry, antiques, and so forth—should be appraised by experts.

Managing the Assets—Management of assets during probate differs from continuing management by a trustee. The personal representative's primary investment responsibilities are to preserve the assets and determine which assets need to be sold to provide liquidity. Once the cash needs in an estate have been determined, the personal representative must develop a schedule for the timely liquidation of assets to provide the cash necessary to meet estate liquidity needs. The probate laws of many states have been liberalized to enable personal representatives to actively manage securities. This allows experienced money managers to make investment decisions based on the needs of the beneficiaries rather than solely on cash needs in the estate. If the estate contains a business interest, the personal representative must either continue to manage that business, liquidate, or sell. If the decision is to continue the business, it may be necessary to hire on-site management. The selection of a manager may be a complex and time-consuming procedure. If a decision is made to sell, several appraisals may be necessary to assure the estate of receiving a fair price.

Paying Creditors—One of the personal representative's first duties is to publish notice to creditors. Creditors usually have a specified period of time subsequent to the publishing of notice in which to file claims. The estate cannot be closed during this period of time. Once claims have been submitted, the personal representative must approve, disapprove in whole or in part, or compromise based on his best judgment. If a claim is disapproved, and the creditor brings suit, he will have to defend his position in court. From time to time, claims against an estate will exceed assets. In such situations, the estate is considered to be insolvent. Each state specifies a priority sequence for creditors of insolvent estates. A typical order of priority might be as follows:

1. Mortgages and other specific liens against property.
2. Funeral expenses.
3. Taxes.
4. Judgments in existence at decedent's death.
5. Wages due but unpaid to employees during the year.
6. Medical bills.
7. All other debts—prorata.

In addition to paying creditors, the personal representative must pay the expenses of administration, including his own commission, and out-of-pocket expenses, appraisers' fees, attorneys' fees, and court costs. The personal representative must determine the reasonableness of all claims against the estate.

Determine and Pay Taxes—There are several tax returns the personal representative must prepare during the probate period. The first is a date-of-death income tax return for the decedent. Then there are fiduciary income tax returns for the estate itself. He must also prepare both a federal estate tax return and a state death tax return. The personal representative has a great many opportunities to save taxes for the heirs by making intelligent elections. This is referred to as post mortem (after death) estate planning. An experienced personal representative can often save more than his fee by making the proper elections. A new duty for personal representatives created by the 1976 Tax Reform Act is the determination of cost bases for assets received in a decedent's estate.* Under the old law a decedent's assets obtained a new basis equivalent to their value on the date of death. The effectiveness of the new provision has been postponed to January 1, 1980. Assets acquired after December 31, 1979, will carry your adjusted cost over to your heirs. Assets acquired prior to January 1, 1980, must be valued as of December 31, 1979. Unless you maintain complete and accurate records, the personal representative will have to reconstruct your cost to the best of his ability. This may be a difficult and time-consuming task, thus increasing the cost of administering your estate.

Accounting—In most states, a formal accounting must be filed with the court. In those where a formal accounting is not required, informal accountings should be provided

*Several proposals for changes in carryover basis are currently under consideration. Check with your attorney concerning possible changes and/or further postponements.

to all beneficiaries. The accounting reflects all assets received, debts and taxes paid, and expenses of administration. It should also indicate the plan of distribution.

Distribute—The personal representative's final duty is to distribute the estate assets according to the terms of the will or the laws of intestacy. From time to time the executor will be faced with perplexing problems such as the specific bequest of an item which was not owned by the decedent at the date of death or where there is insufficient cash to meet cash bequests. Most state laws specify how such problems are to be resolved.

SELECTION OF AN EXECUTOR

Most people do not give enough thought to the selection of their executor. The usual choice is a spouse or an adult child. The problem is compounded when the attorney indicates the task is not very onerous and he will be there to help. A spouse or child may do a good job; however, the task is not a simple one. Tax returns must be prepared, legal formalities adhered to, and proper accounting procedures followed. Serious consideration should be given to naming a professional executor. It may well be worth the additional cost to assure that the estate will be handled properly. Also, an inexperienced executor is confronted with personal liabilities of which he may not be aware. For example, the 1976 Tax Reform Act imposes severe penalties on executors who do not provide cost information to beneficiaries within certain time limitations.

There is also the possibility of family conflict. If one child is named to serve, the other children may feel he is getting more than his share. You have probably seen or heard of such situations. Regardless how good a job that child does, he is likely to be criticized by other family members.

A qualified executor can often save more than his fee through efficient and prompt administration, sound investment decisions, and proper use of tax elections. In addition, he will not be involved emotionally and can make impartial decisions concerning estate problems relating to family members. An experienced lawyer could do a good job; however, the lawyer you select may predecease you, be ill, or traveling in a foreign country when your will is being probated. Banks with trust powers and trust companies are in the business of handling estates. They do an excellent job and have the following advantages over any individual:

1. They are always available. Banks do not die, become ill, move away, or take vacations.
2. They have full financial responsibility and their services are backed by millions of dollars of capital; consequently no surety bond is required at the expense of your estate.
3. They are experienced. They know what to do and when to do it with regard to all phases of estate administration.
4. They have specialists with knowledge of investments, real estate, taxes, probate procedure, and so forth available to help on your estate.

Co-Executors—From time to time it might be desirable to name a family member or business associate as a co-executor with a bank or trust company. If that individual has knowledge concerning business operations or unusual assets, he can be of inestimable help to the corporate fiduciary.

CONCLUSION

The probate process can be lengthy, complicated, frustrating, and potentially costly. Estate administration creates responsibilities which most individuals are not prepared to assume. In most instances, your estate will be administered quickly, efficiently, and economically if you nominate a professional representative—either your attorney or a corporate fiduciary.

PART II

ESTATE AND GIFT TAXATION

CHAPTER IV

DEFINING ESTATE AND GIFT TAXATION

There are two areas of taxation on transfers of property: taxes on lifetime transfers (gifts) and taxes on transfers at death. Most states assess gift taxes on transfers during life and some form of death tax on transfers at death. The federal government on the other hand imposes a "unified transfer tax" related to the cumulative value of gifts during lifetime and at death. The unified transfer tax is a combination of a gift tax and an estate tax.

All state tax laws are somewhat different; consequently it would be impractical for us to try to discuss them in any detail. Most planners pay less attention to state death taxes than they do to federal estate taxes; however, in estates under $200,000, the state death tax will usually be greater than the federal tax. Let's look at two situations involving $200,000 estates. Mr. Golden Aspen, a Colorado resident, leaves his estate outright to Mrs. Aspen. There would be no federal estate tax; however, Colorado would assess Mrs. Aspen with a tax of $8,250. Mr. Red Woods, a California resident, leaves his estate outright to his two children. His estate would be subject to an estate tax of $6,600 and a California inheritance tax of $9,200.

INHERITANCE TAX VS. ESTATE TAX

An estate tax is a tax based on the decedent's right to dispose of his property and is assessed against the total estate. An inheritance tax is a tax based on a beneficiary's right to receive property and is assessed against that beneficiary's proportionate share of the estate. Certain exemptions, credits, and deductions may reduce the taxable interest under either type of tax. States which have inheritance taxes usually allow exemptions based on the relationship of the beneficiary to the decedent. The closer the relationship, the higher the exemption and the lower the tax.

To illustrate the distinction between an estate tax and an inheritance tax, assume Mr. Max Levy dies leaving a $100,000 estate one-half to his wife, Min, and one-half to his son, Norm. If an estate tax were imposed it would be a percentage of the total estate. An estate tax rate of 7.5%, for example, would result in a tax of $7,500. An inheritance tax as you will recall is based on the relationship of each beneficiary. Min, for example, might be entitled to a $25,000 exemption with the balance taxed at 10% for a tax of $2,500 while Norm receives only a $10,000 exemption and has the balance of his inheritance taxed at 12.5% for a tax of $5,000.

THE UNIFIED TRANSFER TAX

Prior to January 1, 1977, the Internal Revenue Code provided for separate estate and gift tax rates. The gift tax rate was approximately three-quarters of the estate tax rate. Effective January 1, 1977, the old estate and gift tax rates were replaced by a single unified rate schedule which is applied to the *cumulative* value of all taxable lifetime gifts *and* transfers at death.

Under prior law certain exemptions were allowed for both gift and estate tax purposes. Under the new law there are no exemptions. Those exemptions have been replaced by a single unified credit. The distinction between an exemption and a credit is that an exemption is deducted from the taxable amount before calculating the tax and a credit is deducted from the tax itself.

*Example:**	Exemption under old law	Credit under new law
	$200,000	$200,000
Exemption	60,000	-0-
	140,000	200,000
X Tax rate	.30	.30
Tax	42,000	60,000
Credit	-0-	30,000
Payable	$42,000	$30,000

THE UNIFIED CREDIT

The new credit results in a substantial reduction of taxes for most estates; consequently it was necessary to phase it in over a period of time in order to soften the impact on government revenues. The following schedule illustrates how it was phased in:

Death Occurs in:	*Amount of Credit Allowed*
1977	30,000
1978	34,000
1979	38,000
1980	42,500
1981 and thereafter	47,000

The $47,000 unified credit is equivalent to an exemption of $175,625. In effect, this means there will be no estate tax payable on estates under $175,625 from 1981 on. This is a substantial increase over the former $60,000 exemption.

*This example is illustrative only and not intended to reflect the actual tax consequences in a $200,000 estate.

CHAPTER V

TAXATION OF LIFETIME GIFTS

The unified transfer tax has severely limited our opportunities for reducing estate taxes through lifetime transfers; however, there are still several important reasons to consider transferring property to your heirs during your lifetime. The transfer of appreciating assets, common stock, or real estate, for example, will shift future appreciation out of your estate into the estate of your donee. If you are in a relatively high income tax bracket, you can make gifts of income-producing assets and shift taxable income to family members who might be in lower brackets.

THE ANNUAL EXCLUSION

You can give $3,000 per year to as many individuals (donees) as you want without those gifts being subjected to any federal tax. For example, a grandparent with fourteen grandchildren can transfer $42,000 per year to those grandchildren free of tax. If his estate is in the 37% bracket ($500,000 to $750,000), he will decrease his ultimate tax bill $15,540 per year by making these gifts. Depending on individual state laws, there may be some state gift tax to pay on these transfers.

PRESENT VS. FUTURE INTEREST GIFTS

In order to qualify for the annual exclusion, a transfer must be a gift of a present interest. A present-interest gift is one in which the donee has an immediate right of possession and enjoyment. A gift of a future interest is one in which enjoyment is delayed until some future date. Obviously an outright gift of cash, securities, or other property falls into the category of a present-interest gift, but many people do not want to make outright gifts. What other types of gifts qualify as gifts of a present interest?

GIFTS IN TRUST

The beneficiaries of a trust are considered to be the donees of the gift and not the trust itself. A gift in trust with income to A for life, principal to B, creates both a present and a future interest. A's right to receive income is a present interest and B's right to principal (the assets of the trust), a future interest. The value of each interest is determined actuarially based upon the beneficiary's life expectancy. If A is fifty years old, the value of his present interest is .67997. If the gift in trust totaled $10,000, $6,799.70 would be treated as a present-interest gift to A. The balance of $3,200.30 would be treated as a future-interest gift to B.

GIFTS TO MINORS

Gifts of items other than cash to minors create numerous problems. If a parent transfers listed securities or real property into his children's names, those assets cannot be sold unless a legal guardian is appointed to act on each child's behalf. A guardian would be required to post bond and report to the court periodically, which could result in expenses that would offset any tax savings resulting from the gifts.

GIFTS TO MINORS ACT

Many states have enacted gifts to minors acts which enable a donor to make gifts to a custodian for the benefit of a minor and avoid the necessity for a guardianship. This is an effective way to make relatively small gifts of securities and cash to minors. Most states also allow gifts of life insurance; however, only two, Connecticut and Washington, permit real property to be transferred to a custodian.

The income from custodial property is normally taxed to the minor; however, if it is used to discharge a legal obligation of the parent to provide support, it will be taxed to the parent. Another word of caution: the donor should not be the custodian. Even though the gift, when made, would qualify as a completed gift and be subject to gift taxation, the I.R.S. has taken the position that the asset will be included in the donor-custodian's estate when he passes away on the theory he maintained control over the asset.

TRUSTS FOR MINORS

Most people prefer not to allow children to have access to substantial funds at too early an age; consequently, large gifts to minors are usually made in trust. Such gifts will be treated as present-interest gifts if the trust distributes outright to the child when he attains age twenty-one and certain other conditions are met.

Many donors believe distributions should be withheld beyond age twenty-one to a point when the beneficiary might be more mature. As a consequence, a trust is created for the minor beneficiary's lifetime, requiring the income to be distributed to him or for his benefit. Under this type of trust, the present-interest gift (amount qualifying for the annual exclusion) is calculated actuarially based on the child's life expectancy. Because of the relatively long life expectancy, almost the entire amount transferred into the trust will qualify as a present-interest gift. The present-interest portion of a lifetime trust for a boy age thirteen is .93708. Trusts of this type are often funded over a period of years taking advantage of many annual exclusions.

The donor should *not* be trustee under this type of trust. If he is, the trust assets will probably be included in his estate under the theory he reserved the right to alter, amend, revoke, or terminate the trust. The safest approach is to name an independent third party as trustee; however, if that trustee charges a fee the tax advantage in early years may be mitigated.

GIFT SPLITTING

Any gift made by either spouse may be treated as if each spouse contributed one-half as long as the non-donor spouse consents. If, for example, A makes a gift of $6,000 to B and A's wife consents to making it a split gift, A will be considered to have made a $3,000 gift and Mrs. A will be considered to have made a $3,000 gift. If any gift is split during a particular calendar year, all gifts must be split. In a previous example, we had a grandfather make gifts of $42,000 to his fourteen grandchildren. If the grandmother joins in on the gift, he can give them $84,000 each year and pay no federal gift tax.

GIFT TAX MARITAL DEDUCTION

The gift tax marital deduction provides that the first $100,000 of gifts in excess of $3,000 per year from one spouse to another is free of gift tax. The next $100,000 of gifts in excess of $3,000 per year is fully taxable and 50% of all interspousal gifts in excess of $200,000 are deductible.

VALUATION OF THE GIFT AND COST BASIS TO THE DONEE

The value of a gift for purposes of the unified transfer tax is the market value on the date of transfer. The donee's basis for purposes of determining the taxable gain on a subsequent sale is the donor's cost increased by the amount of tax attributable to the gift. For example, assume Ben E. Factor gives his son, Mel, stock valued at $10,000. Ben paid $5,000 for that stock many years ago. As a result of making this gift, Ben paid a $500 gift tax. A year later the stock appreciates to $12,000 and Mel sells it. His taxable gain would be $6,500 calculated as follows:

Sales price		$12,000
Cost:		
Ben's cost	$5,000	
Tax on gift	500	
Mel's cost		5,500
Gain on sale		$6,500

For purposes of determining loss, the donee's basis is the lower of the fair market value at the time of the gift or the donor's cost adjusted for the tax paid. For example, assume Ben gives Mel additional stock with a fair market value of $6,000, but Ben paid $8,000 for the stock and incurred gift taxes of $300. Mel subsequently sells the stock for $7,000. He cannot take a loss on the sale for income tax purposes because the fair market value at the date of the gift was less than the sales price. The moral of this example is to give away appreciated assets and not assets which have declined in value.

Valuation of real property, closely held stock, art objects, and other unique assets are subject to close scrutiny by the tax authorities. For your protection, it is advisable to have this type of asset appraised by a qualified appraiser prior to making the gift. The general rule for determining a reasonable value is what a willing buyer will give a willing seller.

GIFTS OF PAST OR FUTURE EARNINGS

You cannot make a gift of taxable income to a donee and avoid income tax. A life insurance agent, for example, is entitled to renewal commissions which he can legally assign to a third party; however, those commissions will be taxable to the agent. The most common object of a gift which incurs adverse income tax consequences is the U.S. Government Series E Bond. When a Series E Bond is given away, any accrued interest which has not previously been reported by the donor must be included in his current year's income tax return. The interest will be taxable to the donor even if he donates the bonds to charity.

Care must be taken not to make gifts of any assets which include an element of taxable income unless the donor is in a relatively low tax bracket. In most cases gifts of this type would be impractical.

GIFTS MADE WITHIN THREE YEARS OF DEATH

All gifts in excess of $3,000 per person per year made within three years prior to death are automatically includible in the donor's taxable estate. Any taxes paid as a result of these gifts are also added to the donor's estate. Taxable gifts in excess of $3,000 made more than three years prior to the donor's death are added to his taxable estate, but the tax paid on such gifts is not taken into consideration.

To illustrate how these rules work, assume Mrs. Dorothy Donor gives her daughter, Dolly, $250,000 over a two-year period. After making the gifts and paying the taxes, Dorothy has assets of $700,000 in her name. In illustration I, Dorothy is assumed to have died within three years of the last gift. In illustration II, she is assumed to have died more than three years after the gifts were made.

	I Death Occurs within 3 years		II Death Occurs in fourth year	
Gifts	$250,000		$250,000	
Exclusions	6,000		6,000	
Net includible gifts		$244,000		$244,000
Gift tax included		26,300		-0-
		$270,300		$244,000
Dorothy's estate at death		700,000		700,000
Tentative tax base		$970,300		$944,000

Obviously, the inclusion of gift taxes paid is only a problem in relatively large estates. After 1981, no federal gift tax will be incurred until total taxable gifts exceed $175,000 as a result of the unified credit.

Split gifts during the three-year period receive unique treatment. The surviving spouse's share of split gifts made during this period including the $3,000 exclusion is fully taxable in the donor spouse's estate. Gifts joined in by the surviving spouse more than three years prior to the donor spouse's death escape taxation completely in the donor spouse's estate.

CONCLUSION

While the tax advantages of lifetime gifts have been reduced as a result of the unified transfer tax, they can still be useful in planning larger estates. Annual exclusions, marital deductions, and gift splitting continue to provide for savings as do gifts of income-producing and -appreciating properties.

CHAPTER VI

TAXATION OF TRANSFERS AT DEATH

Transfers at death trigger several tax consequences. The most well known are inheritance taxes and estate taxes. The least well known is taxation of income in respect of decedent (IRD). There is also one relatively new consequence resulting from the Tax Reform Act of 1976: Carryover Basis. This chapter will provide you with an understanding of the basics of these concepts.

INCOME IN RESPECT OF DECEDENT

Many individuals are entitled to taxable income which has not been received prior to their death. A doctor's accounts receivable and an insurance agent's renewal commissions are examples of IRD.

IRD is included in a decedent's taxable estate for death tax purposes. It is also subject to income taxation as received by the heirs. This appears to be double taxation, and it is; however, as income taxes are assessed a deduction is allowed for estate taxes previously paid.

To qualify for the estate tax deduction, IRD must be among those assets on which the estate tax is assessed. If it is given to a spouse as part of the marital deduction, for example, it will not be entitled to the special deduction for income tax purposes.

CARRYOVER BASIS AND FRESH START*

Prior to the 1976 Tax Reform Act, assets acquired a new capital gain tax basis when death occurred equivalent to their fair market value as of the date of death. Now all assets retain the decedent's cost adjusted only for death taxes; however, all property which the decedent owns on December 31, 1979, receives a "fresh start" equivalent to its value on that date.

All listed securities will have as their "fresh start" basis the mean between their high and low price on December 31, 1979. All other assets are subject to a special valuation method which assumes appreciation occurs at a uniform rate from the date of acquisition to the date of death. Under the special valuation method the fresh start is calculated by multiplying the appreciation from date of acquisition to date of death by a ratio representing the number of days the decedent owned the property before January 1, 1980, divided by the total number of days he held the property. If depreciation, depletion, or amortization has been allowed, it must be added back to the tax basis in determining the amount of appreciation.

> **Example:** Miss Tess Tater bought an apartment house on January 1, 1956, for $200,000. She made very few improvements to the property, but upon the date of her death, January 1, 1981, the apartment house was appraised to be worth $300,000. Over the twenty-five-year period she wrote off $100,000 of depreciation. The fresh start basis is calculated as follows:
>
> Step one: Determine total appreciation:
>
> Market value January 1, 1981 $300,000

*Several proposals for changes in carryover basis are currently under consideration. Check with your attorney concerning possible changes and/or further postponements.

Less:		
Tax basis	$100,000	
Depreciation	100,000	
Adjusted basis		200,000
Total appreciation		$100,000

Step two: Determine the ratio of days owned prior to 1-01-80 as related to the total days owned:

$$\frac{8766}{9131} = .96003$$

Step three: Multiply the total appreciation by the ratio to determine appreciation prior to 1-01-80

$100,000 × .96003 = $96,003

Step four: Multiply the total depreciation by the ratio to determine depreciation allowed prior to 1-01-80

$100,000 × .96003 = $96,003

Step five: Calculate fresh start basis by adding the pre-1980 appreciation and depreciation to the pre-death tax basis

Tax basis	$100,000
Appreciation	96,003
Depreciation	96,003
Fresh start	$292,006

A minimum carryover basis of $60,000 will be allowed in all estates; consequently if an individual's estate consists of securities valued at $100,000 for which he paid $10,-000, his heirs will be entitled to use the minimum basis of $60,000 in calculating any gain. In addition, up to $10,-000 of household and personal effects are exempt from the carryover basis rule.

ADJUSTMENT FOR DEATH TAXES PAID

The carryover basis can be increased to reflect federal and state death taxes in the same ratio that net appreciation in that property bears to the fair market value of all property subject to the tax.

Example: Assume Tess in our prior example had a total estate of $500,000 and her estate paid total taxes of $25,000. Using the formula described above, the carryover basis would be increased by $4,800 to $296,806.

$$\frac{\$96{,}003}{\$500{,}000} \times \frac{\text{Basis increase}}{\$25{,}000}$$

Basis increase = $4,800

EXTENSIONS FOR PAYMENT OF TAX

The IRS can allow an extension of up to ten years if the personal representative can show "reasonable cause." This can give the personal representative the time necessary to convert investment assets to cash.

If the decedent's estate contains a closely held business the value of which exceeds 35% of his gross estate or 50% of his taxable estate, his personal representative can obtain a ten-year extension.

If a closely held business or farm represents 65% of the decedent's adjusted gross estate, payment of the estate tax can be deferred completely for five years and then paid in ten equal installments. If the decedent had interests in more than one business, they can be aggregated for the 65% test; however, he must have had at least a 20% interest in each such company.

One of the frightening aspects of these extensions is that the tax can be accelerated if a payment is not made when due or if as much as one-third of the business is disposed of. These provisions could force a sale at a very inappropriate time to the disadvantage of the heirs. Taxes should normally be paid as soon as possible to avoid this type of problem.

The regular rate of interest on deferred payments at this writing is 6%; however, a special 4% rate is allowed on the estate tax attributable to the first $1,000,000 of farm property or closely held business interests.

THE ESTATE TAX MARITAL DEDUCTION

When a married person dies, his estate is allowed a deduction for certain property interests passing to his surviving spouse. This deduction will be the greater of $250,000 or 50% of his adjusted gross estate. The adjusted gross estate is the total estate less all debts and estate settlement costs. The following illustration identifies the advantage of the marital deduction in a $600,000 estate.

	No Marital Deduction	Marital Deduction Available
Gross estate	$600,000	$600,000
Less settlement costs, etc.	60,000	60,000
Adjusted gross estate	540,000	540,000
Less marital deduction	-0-	270,000
Taxable estate	$540,000	$270,000
Gross estate tax	$170,000	$77,600
Less: unified tax credit	47,000	47,000
Estate tax payable	$123,000	$30,600

(The taxes would be greater for deaths occurring prior to 1981 due to the graduated unified tax credit.)

Community Property—Prior to the 1976 Tax Reform Act, there was no marital deduction for community property. This was logical because each spouse owned a one-half interest in the community and only one-half was taxed when a spouse died. The $250,000 minimum marital deduction would have created an inequity favoring people with separate property unless it was extended to community property; consequently the act provides that in community estates under $500,000 an amount can be passed free of tax to the surviving spouse to provide the equivalent of a $250,000 marital deduction.

For example, assume Mr. and Mrs. Marital Bliss have a community estate of $450,000. Under community property laws, each is presumed to own one-half or $225,000. If Mr. Bliss dies he can leave his wife $25,000 of his estate tax free ($225,000 + 25,000 = $250,000). The remaining $200,000 of his estate would be subject to tax.

Survivorship—In order to obtain the marital deduction, the inheriting spouse must in fact survive under the law. Where it is impossible to determine which spouse passed away first, such as in a common accident, the law of the state or provisions (simultaneous death clause) in the document (will, trust, life insurance policy, and so forth) making disposition of the property will govern.

A simultaneous death clause should be included in the document whenever it is important to obtain the marital deduction. This is a clause which states, in effect, "If my wife and I die under circumstances where it is impossible to determine who died first, my wife shall be deemed to have survived me."

A logical question for you to ask might be "Why wouldn't everyone want to take advantage of the marital deduction?" There are tax advantages to not using the marital deduction when both spouses have large estates but one estate is considerably larger than the other. If the estate of the surviving spouse is substantially greater than that of the first spouse to die, use of the marital deduction would result in excessive taxes upon the survivor's death.

> **Example:** George and Mary Rich are married and have two children. Mary inherited $500,000 from her parents some years ago and George has accumulated an estate of $200,000. Upon George's death, he could pass his estate to Mary free of tax due to the marital deduction; however, his attorney sug-

gests he by-pass Mary and distribute directly to the children to obtain the following tax savings:

With the marital deduction

George's estate	$200,000	
Less marital ded.	250,000	
Taxable estate	-0-	
Distribute to Mary	$200,000	
Mary's personal assets	500,000	
Mary's estate		$700,000
Gross estate tax	229,800	
Less unified credit	47,000	
Estate tax payable		182,800
Total to children		$517,200

Without the marital deduction

George's estate		$200,000	
Gross estate tax	$54,800		
Less: unified credit	47,000		
Estate tax payable		7,800	
Distribute to children			$192,200
Mary's estate		500,000	
Gross estate tax	155,800		
Less unified credit	47,000		
		108,800	
Distributable to children			391,200
Total to children			583,400
Tax Savings			$66,200

Transfers Which Qualify for the Marital Deduction—Any asset which passes outright to the surviving spouse qualifies for the marital deduction. Bequests under the deceased spouse's will, life insurance proceeds payable to the survivor, and joint tenancy property are all examples of property passing outright to the surviving spouse. In addition to property which passes outright, certain restricted interests can also qualify. Among these are the marital deduction trust and certain annuities.

The main consideration is whether or not the restricted transfer represents a "terminable interest" because such an interest will not qualify for the marital deduction. A terminable interest is one in which the survivor may not have continuing enjoyment of the asset during his lifetime and the right to dispose of the remainder interest in that asset upon his death to whomever he desires. Examples of terminable interests include trusts in which the income goes to the surviving spouse and the principal to his children or an annuity in which any remainder interest goes to a third party.

ORPHANS' EXCLUSION

If a minor child has no known surviving parent and the decedent has no surviving spouse, the estate is entitled to a deduction equal to $5,000 multiplied by the excess of twenty-one over the child's age on the date of the decedent's death.

> **Example:** Mr. and Mrs. Angel are killed in an airplane crash while vacationing in Europe. Their three-year-old son and five-year-old daughter survive. Under the orphans' exclusion, their son can receive $90,000 and their daughter $80,000 free of federal estate tax. These amounts are calculated as follows:
>
> Son's deduction = (21 − 3) × $5,000 = 18 × $5,000 = $90,000
> Daughter's deduction = (21 − 5) × $5,000 = 16 × $5,000 = $80,000

The above deduction applies to any interest which passes to or has passed to the child. If gifts were made during the parent's lifetime, those gifts would be added to any bequests in determining the deductible amount.

If one spouse passes away and the surviving spouse remarries, upon that surviving spouse's death no orphans' exclusion will be allowed because he will be survived by his new spouse.

Normally a legal adoption will supplant a blood relationship for purposes of this deduction; however, this will not be the case if the adoption was motivated for the purpose of obtaining the deduction. For example, a child who was put up for adoption through normal channels by his natural parents and whose adopted parents die can qualify. On the other hand, an aunt or uncle who is terminally ill cannot adopt a child solely for the purpose of obtaining the deduction.

Property does not have to pass outright to the minor in order to obtain the deduction. The rules relating to restricted gifts for marital deduction purposes generally apply to the orphans' exclusion; however, the property can pass to a third person if the orphan dies before the youngest child of the decedent attains age twenty-one. In other words, a qualifying gift in trust for two children of the decedent can pass to any third party if those children do not survive distribution with no adverse consequence. If only one of the children dies, his share can go to the other child with no adverse tax consequence. The orphans' exclusion presents some unique planning problems inasmuch as each child of a different age will receive a different amount. Documents must be drafted carefully to assure equitable distribution among all the children. Once again this points out the importance of having a competent estate planning attorney work with you in implementing your estate plan.

RESTRICTIONS ON GENERATION SKIPPING

People of substance, like the Rockefellers and Duponts, have historically avoided estate taxes over many generations by creating what have been referred to as generation-skipping trusts. Typically, the settlor of a generation-skipping trust would name his children as income beneficiaries and provide for the principal to pass to the grandchildren. There would be an estate tax imposed upon the settlor's death, but no tax when the children die.

The Tax Reform Act of 1976 placed severe restrictions on generation skipping. First, the law provides that each generation will be taxed, but there will be only one tax per generation. In other words, if a settlor leaves property in trust for two sons, and upon the first son's death the property passes to the trust for the second son, there will be a tax on the first son's death; however, when the second son passes away the property will pass to his heirs free of tax.

Second, there is a special $250,000 exclusion for each child covering transfers to grandchildren.

> **Example:** Skip Jenner has an after tax estate of $1,500,000. He leaves the estate in a generation-skipping trust for the benefit of his three children, Art, Bob, and Cal. Art has one child, Bob has two, and Cal is married but has no children. Upon Art's death $250,000 will pass to his child free of tax. Upon Bob's death $125,000 will pass to each of his children free of tax. Upon Cal's death the entire amount passing to his wife will be taxable. The $250,000 exclusion applies only to property passing to grandchildren.

The above rules apply only to transfers occurring after April 30, 1976. Transfers emanating from irrevocable trusts in existence on that date are non-taxable. Wills and trusts executed before May 1, 1976, and not subsequently amended, receive special dispensation through January 1, 1982. If a settlor or testator passes away during that period, the old rules will apply. If your will was written prior to May 1, 1976, and contains a generation-skipping provision, your attorney may recommend it not be changed until January 1, 1982, in order to preserve the tax advantage.

WHAT ASSETS ARE INCLUDED IN YOUR TAXABLE ESTATE?

As a general rule, all assets over which you have a right of disposition or which you have previously given away will be considered for inclusion in your estate when you pass away. It would be impossible to cover all possibilities in the space provided; however, the most common includible property interests will be discussed.

Assets in your name alone—All assets in your name alone are fully taxable unless your personal representative can prove you were holding title as either a nominee or trustee for some third party.

Assets Held in Joint Tenancy or Tenancy By the Entirety—Generally, the entire value of jointly owned property is includible in your taxable estate except to the extent the surviving joint tenant can prove contribution. There is one exception to this general rule which applies to joint tenancies involving spouses. The law provides for a "qualified joint interest" which results in only one-half of the joint tenancy property being included in the decedent's estate regardless of which spouse furnished the consideration.

A qualified joint interest is created as follows:

1. The interest must have been created by the decedent, the decedent's spouse, or both subsequent to December 31, 1976.
2. Personal property transferred into joint tenancy must be a completed gift for gift tax purposes.
3. If the joint interest is in real property, the donor must elect to treat the creation of the joint tenancy as a taxable gift at the time title is taken as joint tenants.

COMMUNITY PROPERTY

As was discussed in an earlier chapter, community property is property acquired by either spouse during the marriage except by gift or inheritance. Only one-half of the community property is included in the deceased spouse's estate.

LIFE INSURANCE

The proceeds of life insurance on your life are included in your taxable estate if the policy is payable to the estate, you own the policy, or you simply possess some incident of ownership at the time of your death. The right to change beneficiaries or even to revise the method of settlement are sufficient incidents of ownership to result in the proceeds being taxable.

The tax collector will do everything in his power to include life insurance proceeds in your estate regardless of who the owner of the policies might be. If ownership of a policy is transferred to a third party within three years prior to your death, the entire proceeds will be included in your taxable estate (less the $3,000 annual exclusion). A portion of the policy may be included if you continue to directly or indirectly pay premiums more than three years after the transfer of said policy.

ANNUITIES

Annuities purchased by the decedent which continue on for the benefit of another party are included in the decedent's estate. The amount included is the actuarial value of payments that will be made after his death. Assume Pa Tee and Ann Tee purchased a joint and survivor annuity when Pa was sixty-five and Ann sixty-four. Payments for their joint lifetimes were $693.40 per month. Pa died at age seventy. Ann's life expectancy at age sixty-nine is 12.5 years. The present value of $693.40 per month for 12.5 years is approximately $100,000, which is included in Pa's taxable estate.

If the annuity was totally or partially purchased by someone else, the trustee under a profit sharing plan, for example, only the value attributed to the decedent's contribution is included.

RETIREMENT BENEFITS (PENSION, PROFIT SHARING, KEOGH, AND IRA PLANS)

Corporate Pension and Profit Sharing Plans—Death benefits attributable to employer contributions will be excluded from the decedent's estate if they are paid in installments and are not payable to the decedent's estate. Lump sum distributions and benefits attributable to the decedent's contributions are fully taxable.

> **Example:** Mr. R. E. Tyre has participated in a qualified retirement plan in which his company contributed $2 for every dollar he contributed. At the time of his death, the benefits could be paid out in a lump sum of $150,000 or payable to his widow over her lifetime. If payable in a lump sum, $150,000 would be included in his estate. If payable in installments, only the portion attributable to the decedent's contribution, $50,000, will be included in his taxable estate.

Keogh Plans (Self-Employed Retirement Plans)—The same general rule which applies to corporate plans also applies to Keogh Plans. The benefits attributable to contributions for which tax deductions were obtained are excludible.

IRA Plans (Individual Retirement Accounts)—Same as Keogh Plans.

While it appears advisable for benefits to be paid to beneficiaries in installments this may not always be the case. As each installment is received, it will be treated as ordinary income. On the other hand, a lump sum distribution will benefit from a special ten-year income-averaging provision.

If the decedent was married, inclusion of the death benefit will also tend to increase the marital deduction, thus reducing the estate tax impact.

INTERESTS IN TRUSTS

Trusts Created By the Decedent—Any trust created by the decedent in which he retained a right to the income will be included in his estate. The I.R.S. will also attempt to include any trust which the decedent created for the benefit of another if he retained any element of control over that trust. For example, if the decedent creates a trust for the benefit of a child and names himself trustee, the I.R.S. will try to include the assets of the trust in his taxable estate.

Trusts in Which the Decedent Has a Vested Remainder Interest—If some other person creates a trust in which the decedent or his estate is named as a remainderman, the present value of that remainder interest may be included in the decedent's estate for estate tax purposes.

> **Example:** Assume Mr. Ernest Money created a trust under his will from which Mrs. Money receives the income but principal is to be paid to his son, Bill, or Bill's estate. Bill predeceased his mother, who is age sixty-seven at the time of Bill's death. The trust has a value of $500,000. The value of Bill's remainder interest based on his mother's age is .54542 or $272,-710. This is the amount which would be included in Bill's estate as a vested remainder interest.

Vested remainders are often ignored in estate planning. As you can see, they can make a significant difference in any estate and may create liquidity problems for the decedent's family. One situation which remains vivid in my memory involved a man who died leaving a young family and very little in the way of productive assets. For tax purposes, his estate included a $1,000,000 remainder interest in a trust. There was no way taxes could be paid nor was there any way in which his family could benefit. Fortunately, taxes can be postponed until the trust distributes, but that may be many years. In the interim, this young man's family is destitute.

POWERS OF APPOINTMENT

A general power of appointment exercisable upon death is generally includible in the holder's estate unless it is exercisable in conjunction with an adverse party. Special or limited powers are not includible.

GIFTS MADE DURING LIFE

All gifts over and above those qualifying for the annual exclusion made after September 8, 1976, will be brought back into the estate in calculating the unified transfer tax.

The foregoing discussion covers the most common property interests included in a decedent's taxable estate. You may have other taxable interests. Your attorney will normally be able to advise you concerning what types of property interests might be includible in your estate.

CHAPTER VII

VALUATION OF PROPERTY FOR GIFT AND ESTATE TAX PURPOSES

Fair market value is the criterion normally used to evaluate property for gift and estate tax purposes. The fair market value of listed securities is relatively easy to ascertain from your local newspaper. The specific value used is the mean between the high and low sales prices on the date of death or gift. The "bid" price is used for unlisted securities and mutual funds. Antiques, jewelry, collections, and so forth must be appraised by qualified appraisers. Businesses are usually valued at what a willing buyer will pay to a willing seller. This usually requires an appraiser; however, an arm's-length purchase agreement entered into prior to death can establish a value if certain criteria are met. Real property is normally valued at its highest and best use. Once again an appraiser is necessary to establish that value. The foregoing represents general rules for valuation. Now let's look at some exceptions to these rules.

VALUATION OF LARGE BLOCKS OF STOCK

Periodically, an individual will die holding a substantial amount of stock in a major company. The personal representative may evaluate the stock below its market value on the premise that if all the stock were sold at the same time, it would depress the market significantly. This premise, called the "blockage" rule, has been accepted as a valid approach to valuing large blocks of stock.

MINORITY INTERESTS IN CLOSELY HELD BUSINESSES

A minority stockholder in a closely held corporation has very little authority or control, and there is a limited market for his stock. It may be possible to argue that this stock is worth less than the fair market value.

SPECIAL VALUATION OF REAL PROPERTY USED IN FARMING OR CLOSELY HELD BUSINESSES

One factor commonly used in valuing real property is the value if that property were put to its "highest and best" use. A farm property, for example, might be in a rapidly developing area and be ideally suited for a shopping center or residential development. Its highest and best use would be as one of these types of developments and not as a farm.

The Tax Reform Act of 1976 allows the personal representative to elect to value real estate used in farming or a closely held business based on its *actual use* rather than its highest and best use if the following criteria are met:

1. The decedent must be a United States citizen or resident.
2. The property itself must be located in the United States.
3. The property was being used as a farm or in a business on the date of the decedent's death.
4. At least 50% of the gross estate less expenses, mortgages, and indebtedness consists of *real or personal* property which was being used as a farm or business on the date of the decedent's death.

5. The property must pass to or for the benefit of a family member. It can be held in trust for family members rather than passing outright and still qualify.
6. At least 25% of the decedent's gross estate consists of real property which was given to a family member prior to death or passed to a family member after death, and meets the following requirements:

   a. The real property was owned and used as a farm or business by the decedent or a member of his family for a total of at least five years during the eight-year period immediately preceding his death.
   b. There was material participation by the decedent or a member of his family in the operation of the farm or business for a total of at least five years during the eight years immediately preceding his death. If a farm was leased to a tenant farmer, for example, for four years, it would not qualify.

7. When the personal representative makes this election, he must file an agreement which specifies the property and is signed by all persons having an interest in the property consenting to the potential penalties involved if the property is disposed of or ceases to be used in the farm or business during the following fifteen years.

DISPOSITION OR FAILURE TO USE PROPERTY FOR A QUALIFIED USE

If within fifteen years after the decedent's death one of the heirs sells or transfers the property to a non-family member or he ceases to use it for farming or other closely held business purposes, the additional estate tax based on highest and best use becomes due and payable.

The full amount of the tax is payable if the property fails to qualify during the first ten years. If the property fails to qualify after the tenth year, the tax will be ratably reduced. For example, assume the property is sold at the end of the eleventh year. There are sixty months in five years; consequently the additional tax due would be reduced by 12/60 or 20%.

The heir is personally liable for any estate tax due upon cessation of use for farm or business purposes or on nonqualified disposition.

The property does not have to continually qualify during the fifteen-year period, but if there is no material participation by the heirs for a period aggregating three years out of any eight, it will no longer qualify.

VALUATION OF A FARM FOR FARMING PURPOSES

If there is comparable land which has been rented out for farming purposes, the personal representative can apply a formula which divides the average annual gross rental for five years less the average real estate taxes for such land by the average annual effective interest rate for all new federal land bank loans.

$$\frac{\text{5-year average gross rental} - \text{five-year average real estate taxes}}{\text{5-year average federal land bank interest rate}}$$

Assume the average rental is \$50 per acre, the average taxes \$8 per acre, and the average interest rate 7%.

$$\frac{\$50 - \$8}{.07} = \$600 \text{ per acre}$$

If this formula cannot be used because there is no comparable land or where the personal representative elects against using it, the following procedure for real estate held in a closely held business can be used.

VALUATION OF REAL ESTATE IN A CLOSELY HELD BUSINESS

The following factors are to be used in determining the value of qualified real property:

1. The capitalization of income which the property can be expected to yield over a reasonable period of time under prudent management considering traditional cropping patterns, soil capacity, and so forth. The code does not specify a capitalization rate. This would probably depend on economic circumstances at the date of death. Once you have calculated the anticipated income, divide it by the capitalization rate to determine the property value. For example, assume the property could generate $100 per year and a reasonable rate of return would be 12.5%.

   $$\frac{\$100}{.125} = \$800 \text{ per acre}$$

2. The capitalization of the fair rental value of the property for a qualified purpose. Assume the rental value is $50 per acre and a reasonable return on rental property is 10%.

   $$\frac{\$50}{.10} = \$500 \text{ per acre}$$

3. Assessed land values in a state which provides differential or use value assessment for closely held business or farming. For our purposes, let's assume the assessed value is $400 per acre.
4. Comparable sales of other closely held business or farm property in the same geographical area far enough removed from a metropolitan or resort area so that non-agricultural use is not a significant factor.

Let's assume the average comparable sales price is $660 per acre.

5. Any other factor which fairly values the qualified property. A recent purchase by the decedent or offers to buy comparable properties might be examples of other factors.

After taking all of these factors into consideration, the personal representative places a value on the property. One approach might be to take an average of the values obtained by the various methods. Using our example, the average value would be $590 per acre.

Estate taxes can probably be reduced by using the actual use valuation, but the loss of flexibility in dealing with the property and the increased costs incurred in valuing the estate may make it impractical to use the actual use value in all but the extremely large farm and ranch operations. The personal representative must develop the information to make all of the foregoing calculations and make a judgment valuation concerning whether or not the property will continue to be used for a qualified purpose. Many hours of time and many thousands of dollars will be expended in making these determinations.

The maximum reduction from highest and best use applicable to any gross estate will be $500,000. If the estate qualifies for the marital deduction, the effect would be to reduce the tax on only $250,000.

VALUATION OF A CLOSELY HELD BUSINESS

The Internal Revenue Service recognizes no single formula in evaluating a closely held business. The personal representative must use all relevant methods to arrive at a reasonable value. Some of the factors which should be considered are:

1. The history of the business. The company's growth pattern, the degree of risk, and its operating records should all be taken into consideration.
2. The general economic picture. What is the outlook for the economy in general and this industry in particular?
3. The financial condition of the business. Is the business cash heavy or is it overextended?
4. The company's earning capacity. It is advisable to review several years' profit and loss statements in order to obtain a clear picture of earnings growth.
5. Is there good will or other intangible assets? Good will relates to the earnings over and above what would be considered a fair return on invested capital. The company might also have patents or royalty interests which are not yet producing income, but have substantial value.
6. Recent sales of interests in the business to other than family members. This provides an indication of what a willing buyer will pay a willing seller.
7. The price of stock in similar companies which are traded in the open market. It is unusual to find a closely held company which has the same size and attributes of actively traded public companies, but from time to time they do appear and this is probably one of the most valid indications of value.
8. The importance of the decedent to the success of the company. If the decedent was the primary reason for the company's success, it might be possible to discount the value on the assumption the company will be less successful in the future.

Some of the specific approaches to valuation are:

1. Book value.
2. Capitalization of future earnings.
3. Return on capital plus good will.

The personal representative will usually adopt the approach most favorable to the estate and argue hard for that approach.

BOOK VALUE

Book value normally reflects cost and not market value. Book value is your cost less depreciation and various accounting adjustments. It is normally advisable to adjust book value to reflect the current market value of all assets. Real estate, patents, and inventory should all be appraised for this purpose. The personal representative might reduce adjusted book value to reflect the effects of a possible forced sale, but whatever adjusted book value is arrived at will probably be the lowest possible value for estate tax purposes.

CAPITALIZATION OF EARNINGS

One common approach to valuation of going concerns is capitalization of earnings. You often hear people say they will pay five times earnings or ten times earnings for a particular stock. This, in effect, is capitalization of earnings. A person who is willing to pay five times earnings is saying he expects a 20% return on his money. The capitalization rate will depend upon economic conditions at the time of appraisal. It is advisable to average three years earnings before applying the multiplier you want to use.

RETURN ON CAPITAL PLUS GOOD WILL

This approach indicates two elements and applies a portion of earnings to each. Assume we have a company with an adjusted book value of $200,000 that earns $70,000 per year. If a reasonable return on invested capital is 15%, $30,000 of the earnings are attributable to the $200,000 adjusted book value. The remaining $40,000 represents earnings attributable to good will. If it is prudent to capitalize good will at 20%, we find the good will is also worth $200,000 making our hypothetical company worth $400,000.

As was mentioned earlier, the most valid approach to valuation is what a willing buyer will pay a willing seller. If a binding purchase agreement is entered into prior to death allowing a partner or a key man to buy the business at a specific price, that price will hold for valuing the business in the estate.

CONCLUSION

Valuation of farms and closely held businesses is by far the most complicated aspect of estate settlement. The skill and experience of your executor and/or attorney can save your estate many thousands of dollars. On the other hand, if you have an inexperienced executor or attorney, it can cost your estate a considerable amount.

PART III

THE ESTATE PLANNER'S TOOLS

CHAPTER VIII

WILLS AND INTESTACY

Virtually everyone needs a will. This is true whether the estate consists of millions or an automobile and personal effects. A will is the only way you can guarantee certain types of assets will go to the people you want to receive them. If you do not have a will, the laws of intestacy in your state will dictate who is to receive your property.

LAWS OF INTESTACY

The laws of intestacy will vary from state to state. In California, all community property will pass to a surviving spouse; however, the amount of separate property that spouse will receive depends on whether or not the decedent was survived by children or issue of deceased children. If the decedent leaves a surviving spouse and one child, the separate property is divided equally between the two. If the spouse and two or more children survive, the spouse receives one-third and the children two-thirds. If the deceased spouse leaves no issue, the surviving spouse receives one-half and the remaining one-half goes to the parents of the deceased spouse or their issue. The only situation in which a surviving spouse will receive all of the separate property is when the deceased spouse is not survived by issue or immediate family. While each state has laws covering the succession to property upon death, those laws very seldom coincide with our desires.

IMPORTANCE OF WILLS

Many people are under the mistaken impression that if their property is in joint tenancy or they have a living trust, there is no need for a will. In some instances, this may be true; however, in most, a will is essential to dispose of personal items or make disposition of the estate in the event of a simultaneous death.

A few examples may help to illustrate the importance of wills:

> Mrs. Happy Ness, an elderly widow, lived in a modest home filled with fond memories and cherished personal items which she wanted to be shared by her three daughters. In addition, she had several thousand dollars in a joint bank account with her eldest daughter who lived nearby and tried her best to make certain her mother was comfortable.
>
> Happy passed away peacefully in her sleep one night. Under the laws of her state, the three girls would share equally in all assets held in Happy's name at the time of her death. This meant the home, furniture, and personal items would be divided equally. The savings account, however, would go to the oldest daughter as the surviving joint tenant, but she knew her mother's intent and had indicated a willingness to share it with her sisters.
>
> After the funeral, the three sisters returned to the family home to discuss what action needed to be taken and to decide who would receive what. First, the sisters could not agree on an equitable division of the assets. All three wanted the silver, two wanted the piano. Two wanted the china, and so on and so on. Next, the oldest sister felt she could settle the estate without using an attorney. The other two felt an attor-

> ney should be hired to make certain the probate was properly handled. Finally, while all were agreed the house should be sold, one wanted to try to sell it herself and the others wanted it placed in the hands of a competent real estate broker.
>
> Disagreement followed disagreement and what started off as a friendly meeting ended up in bitterness and confusion. The older sister refused to share the money in the savings account with her younger sisters and each of the three hired her own attorney to protect her interest in the estate. What appeared to be an uncomplicated and inexpensive estate ended up costly, confused, and time consuming.

The majority of these problems could have been resolved if Happy had asked an attorney to write a will indicating what she wanted each daughter to receive and naming an independent executor to administer the estate for her. Situations like this are quite common and should be avoided at any cost.

> Mr. and Mrs. I. N. Love agreed that what little they had belonged to both of them; consequently they put everything they owned in joint tenancy. They did not have wills but felt that when one of them passed away the survivor could make a will. They had discussed the disposition of their estate many times. They had no children, but Mr. Love had an invalid sister and an aged mother who needed all the financial help they could get. Mrs. Love's only living relative was a brother who was an extremely successful businessman. The Loves agreed that the survivor would leave everything to Mr. Love's mother and sister.
>
> Unfortunately, Mr. and Mrs. Love were in a serious automobile accident. Mr. Love was killed immediately, but Mrs. Love was in a coma for several weeks before she died. Mrs. Love as the surviving joint tenant received all of Mr. Love's property and upon her

death, under the laws of intestacy of her state, her brother inherited the entire estate. Mr. Love's mother and sister were unintentionally disinherited.

Proper wills indicating what disposition was to be made of the property upon the survivor's death could have avoided this unfortunate situation.

TYPES OF WILLS

Basically, there are two types of wills: holographic wills and attested wills. A holographic will is a handwritten will. To be valid in most states, it must be written, signed, and dated in the handwriting of the testator (the person making the will). Valid holographic wills have been written on unusual surfaces. For example, an individual injured in an automobile accident used his last ounce of strength to scratch out his will on the fender of his car and that fender was admitted to probate as a valid will.

Handwritten wills have been the source of much litigation. Ambiguous language often results in distribution being made contrary to the testator's desires. I recall one situation in which a spinster schoolteacher who shared her home with a widow friend wrote her own will. In that will, she left her "home and all the contents therein" to the friend. She left the balance of her estate to a niece. At the time of her death, she had $80,000 worth of bonds in the house. Query: were the bonds part of the "contents" or did they go to the niece with the balance of the estate? Maybe, our teacher meant for her friend to receive the bonds, but perhaps her definition of "contents" related only to furniture, furnishings, and personal effects. Unfortunately no one will ever know what she really intended. After many months of litigation and thousands of dollars in attorney's fees the court awarded the bonds to the friend.

Holographic wills should not be witnessed. This converts them from holographic to attested wills and requires they be completed with all the formality of attested wills.

Attested wills are normally typewritten but are not required to be so. The primary requirements of an attested will are that the testator's signature and his capacity to sign be attested to by at least two witnesses (some states require three witnesses). The formalities for witnessing wills vary from state to state; consequently a procedure followed in one state may not be acceptable in another state.

In some states it is not necessary to date your will; however, it is desirable to do so. If two wills are presented for probate, the one with the latest date is usually the one that will be probated. If there is no date, it may be difficult to prove which will is the most recent.

WHAT A WILL CAN DO FOR YOU

Distribute Assets—The most important thing a will can do for you is distribute your assets the way you want them distributed. Not only can you give specific assets to the people you want to receive them but you can also control the point in time when they will receive those assets. For example, you might have a minor child or grandchild to whom you intend to leave a substantial amount of money. If there is a possibility he might receive his inheritance when he is eighteen or twenty-one, he might not yet have the maturity to handle it. Your will can specify that he is not to receive your money until he is somewhat older: twenty-five or thirty, for example. This type of provision in your will is a testamentary trust.

Minimize taxes and provide for their payment—A properly drawn will can help to minimize taxes and other costs in settling your estate. In addition to minimizing taxes, your will can specify whether taxes that are payable should be assessed against each beneficiary's share or paid out of the residue of the estate.

Select an Executor (Personal Representative)—A will enables you to specify who will administer your estate. Without a will, this will be left to the best judgment of the court. The selection of an executor and the responsibilities imposed upon him are discussed in detail in Chapter III.

Select Guardians—You have the right to nominate guardians for your children in your will. Your nomination does not guarantee the court will appoint them to serve; however, it is an indication of your desire and will normally be honored by the court. In the absence of such a nomination any adult member of either spouse's family who is willing to post the required bond could be appointed. A surviving parent is the natural guardian of both the child's property and person. Unless that parent is obviously unfit to serve, he or she will be appointed.

Before continuing with what a will can do for you, let's consider some of the important factors in selection of guardians. The guardian of the person has responsibility for the physical and spiritual well-being of his ward, such as food, shelter, education, discipline, and so forth. The selection of a guardian of the person is extremely sensitive.

Some close family member will undoubtedly be hurt if he or she is not asked to serve; however, you may have a close friend who is more likely to raise your children in the same manner that you would. An older person, your mother for example, may not be physically or emotionally capable of coping with the problems of teenagers. Aunts and uncles may have different lifestyles or have different religious beliefs. The nomination of a guardian of the person is often the most difficult decision to make in estate planning.

The guardian of the property has the duty to manage and preserve the ward's property. This can be a tremendous additional responsibility to place on someone who has never before managed another's property. As was mentioned before, the same person can act as guardian of both the property and the person; however, the individual you select to raise your children may not be a good money manager. If you perceive that he is not handling his own finances properly, he should not be asked to manage money for your children.

Most banks and trust companies are authorized to serve

as property guardians. If the child's potential inheritance is sizable, you may want to consider asking a corporate fiduciary to assist the guardian of the person by managing the child's investments.

In most large communities, qualified individuals are seeking fiduciary appointments of this type. Attorneys who specialize in estate planning will know who these individuals are and apprise you of their capabilities. It is usually advisable to nominate alternate guardians in the event the original nominees are unable or unwilling to act. Most attorneys suggest you ask your proposed guardians, in advance, if they are willing to assume these responsibilities. It might be disastrous if the people you select are unwilling to serve when the need arises.

As you can see, this is not a decision to take lightly. Give it serious thought. Discuss the alternatives with your attorney and other advisors and make certain whatever decision you make will be in the best interests of your children.

Expand Investment Powers—The executor's power to buy and sell is limited in most jurisdictions. For example, the only investment power he might have under a particular state's laws is the power to sell assets in order to raise cash for payment of taxes and other estate settlement costs. In many states, the executor can be given additional powers under the will to enable him to make whatever investment changes he deems necessary to meet the estate's changing requirements.

Waive Bond—Your executor or administrator will be required to post a surety bond and pay the premiums out of your estate. In most states, a statement in your will relieving the executor from posting bond will be honored and should save the estate some money. Banks and trust companies are normally not required to post bond because the courts feel their substantial capital will insure the estate against loss.

WHO SHOULD BE WITNESSES

It is usually a good idea to ask younger people to witness your will. Your contemporaries may pass away before you do and if testimony is needed concerning your capacity or the absence of duress, they would not be available. Signing should take place in your attorney's office to guarantee adherence to all of the formalities of execution.

CODICILS

A codicil is a document written subsequent to the signing of the original will which purports to change some aspect of that will. It must be executed with the same formalities as the will itself.

DISPOSITION OF TANGIBLE PERSONAL PROPERTY

Each of us has certain jewelry, objets d'art, or items of furniture which we would like to leave to specific friends and relatives. Some testators specify each item and the recipient in their wills. Any time a change is required due either to the death of a beneficiary or a change in assets, the will has to be redrawn or a codicil written. The laws of some states allow the testator to refer to a separate list which is not included in the will and which can be changed at the testator's pleasure without rewriting the whole will.

If allocation of assets is left to the discretion of one particular beneficiary, the other beneficiaries who are not able to obtain items they want may feel resentment toward the allocating beneficiary. If the beneficiaries are allowed to pick and choose, frictions can develop among otherwise peaceful friends and relatives.

Deciding how to distribute personal items can be one of the most difficult problems in designing your will. There is usually no problem where there is a surviving spouse or the estate is being divided equally among the children; however, if you want a particular child to receive a particular item, it should be specified. The biggest problems arise in those estates where the beneficiaries are friends and/or distant relatives. The more specific you can be in these situations, the less likely there will be any friction among these individuals.

Another approach is to direct your executor to sell your personal effects and distribute the proceeds among your beneficiaries. If a certain beneficiary wants a particular item, he can use his share of the total proceeds to buy it from the estate.

FUNERAL INSTRUCTIONS

Many people include directions concerning their interment, cremation, organ bequests, and so forth in their wills. It is much more practical for these instructions to be in the hands of your doctor and the people who are most likely to be contacted in the event of your death. It is not uncommon for several days to pass before a will is finally located and, consequently, incorrect disposition of the body may take place.

CONCLUSION

This chapter has covered the disposition of property when a person dies without a will (intestate) and what can be accomplished with a will. It should now be obvious that most, if not all, individuals need wills if to do nothing more than name the person they want to settle their estate or make reasonable distribution of their furniture, furnishings, jewelry, and so forth.

CHAPTER IX

TRUSTS IN GENERAL

The gratification of wealth is not found in mere possession or in lavish expenditures, but in its wise application.
—Cervantes

Trusts are probably the most useful tool in the estate planner's kit. Properly used, they can accomplish almost every objective you might have concerning distribution of your property.

DEFINITION

Basically a trust is an arrangement in which one individual known as the settlor, grantor, creator, or trustor transfers property to a second party known as the trustee who manages that property pursuant to directions of the settlor for the benefit of a third party called the beneficiary.

PARTIES TO THE TRUST

Normally we think only of individuals creating trusts; however, they can also be created by corporations, government entities, and so forth. For our purposes in this chapter, we will discuss only trusts created by individuals.

The trustee can also be a person or a corporation. He has the responsibility for carrying out the terms of the trust. No trust can become functional unless there is a trustee. From time to time a trust is created in which no trustee is named or the person named is unwilling or unable to act. It is a basic tenet of trust law that no trust will fail for want of a trustee; consequently the trust does not terminate when those occasions arise. The trust merely remains inactive until a trustee is found.

The beneficiaries are the people for whom the trust was created. There are two basic types of beneficiaries. The life tenant or income beneficiary receives the income of the trust either during his lifetime or until a specific future date. The beneficiary who receives the principal upon termination is called the remainderman. There can be several income beneficiaries or remaindermen in any particular trust. There can also be successive income beneficiaries. For example, A—the income beneficiary—receives income for life. Upon A's death, B—the successor income beneficiary—gets income for life. Upon B's death, the principal goes to C, the remainderman.

TYPES OF TRUSTS

There are several ways in which trusts can be categorized. First, they can be categorized as either living (intervivos) or testamentary. Living trusts are trusts which are created during your lifetime and testamentary trusts come into existence after your death according to provisions included in your will.

Living Trusts—Living trusts can be either *passive* or *active.* A passive living trust is one in which the document is executed by both the settlor and the trustee, but not funded. No assets are put into a passive trust when it is created other than a possible beneficial interest in life insurance policies. An active trust is one which is funded at the time the document is executed. Living trusts can also be classified as *revocable* or *irrevocable*. A revocable trust is one which the settlor can amend, terminate, activate, or deactivate at any time. An irrevocable trust, on the other hand, cannot be amended or terminated. It can, however, have a specific termination date at which time it can revert back to the settlor or the settlor can have the right to extend the time the trust is to remain irrevocable.

Testamentary Trusts—By far the most common type of trust is the trust created under your will, or the testamentary trust. The primary difference between a testamentary trust and a living trust is that the living trust becomes effective immediately while the testamentary trust does not become effective until the testator dies. In designing the trust, however, it should be assumed the testator will die in the near future. If he survives for several years and his objectives change, he merely writes a new will or executes a codicil to the old one. In most states, testamentary trusts are subject to supervision by the probate court. The trustee is required to report to the court periodically and obtain approval for its actions during the accounting period. This process provides an element of protection to the beneficiaries against mismanagement by the trustee. Testamentary trusts are often more costly to administer because of this court supervision; however, many testators feel the additional protection is worth the additional cost.

THE TRUSTEE

The trustee can be anyone designated by the settlor. The settlor himself can serve as trustee of a living trust which he creates; however, if that trust is irrevocable, it would normally not be advisable for him to serve. Banks and trust companies authorized to act as fiduciaries in each state are often named trustee. Frequently, the settlor will ask his attorney to act. Some settlors will name friends or relatives to serve. Whoever is chosen to serve should have as many of the following qualities as possible:

Honesty—The most important quality for any trustee to have is honesty. He has complete control over all of the assets in the trust. If he can be tempted in any way, the beneficiaries can be hurt.

Investment Ability—While the trustee does not necessarily have to be an investment genius, he should be capable of making the kinds of investment decisions that will help preserve the assets and maximize income.

Impartiality—In some instances a trustee will have to make decisions that favor one beneficiary over another. For example, if a discretionary principal distribution is requested by an income beneficiary, it will reduce the amount the remainderman will receive. The trustee must be able to make this type of decision impartially based on the desires of the trustor as expressed in the trust and the needs of the beneficiary. He should not be prejudiced because he likes or dislikes certain beneficiaries.

Availability—The trustee should be available when he is needed. This is one of the problems with an individual trustee as compared with a corporate trustee. An individual can be traveling when he is needed, he can become incompetent, and he can die. None of these things can happen with a corporate fiduciary.

Financial Responsibility—Regardless of how honest the trustee might be, he should be able to cover any financial losses incurred as a result of his negligence or malfeasance.

As you can see, the choice of a trustee must be carefully made. It is not enough to like and respect an individual. You must be thoroughly convinced that individual will manage your assets for your beneficiaries as you would want him to.

DUTIES OF A TRUSTEE

The restatement of the law of trusts defines a trustee's duties. You should be aware of some of those duties so that you can better appreciate what you are asking of your trustee.

The trust must be administered solely for the best interests of the beneficiaries. No transaction entered into by the trustee should benefit anyone other than the beneficiaries. For example, if the trustee is also a stockbroker, he cannot accept commissions on trust transactions.

A trustee cannot delegate any acts which he can reasonably be required to perform. A corporate fiduciary, for example, must not delegate its investment responsibility to a third party nor should any trustee delegate its power to make discretionary distributions.

Trustees are required to render clear and accurate accounts and provide beneficiaries with whatever information they want concerning the trust. The trustee must also exercise such care and skill as a man of ordinary prudence would exercise in dealing with his own property. If the trustee has greater skill than that of a man of ordinary prudence (an investment counselor, for example), he is under a duty to exercise that greater skill.

Preservation of the trust property is a well-defined duty as is the duty to make trust property productive. If a trustee receives an unproductive asset (raw land, for example), he must make that property productive within a reasonable period of time.

The foregoing duties can be modified by the terms of the trust and other duties can be imposed. Powers and duties are governed first by the trust instrument itself, then by the state law, and finally by case law.

POWERS OF THE TRUSTEE

Trustees should be given broad powers in the trust instrument. If the instrument does not contain certain powers, the trustee may not be able to act as you would want him to.

The typical trust gives the trustee the right to deal with the trust property in the same manner as if it were his own. Where the trustee is given this broad power, he is not subject to the control of the court except to prevent abuses of that power.

Usually the trustee has the right to buy, sell, lease, borrow, make loans, and so forth. In addition, he will be given the power to determine what is income and what is principal. This, along with the power to make discretionary distributions to the various beneficiaries, places the trustee in the same position as the original owner of the property.

From time to time, more than one person is named as trustee. When there is more than one trustee, they are called co-trustees. Co-trustees must exercise the various powers jointly unless the trust instrument specifically relieves one of the trustees from that responsibility.

A third party may have the power to direct the trustee in certain areas. The trustee must follow these directions unless they are to the detriment of the beneficiaries in which case the trustee can refuse to conform. If the person holding the power persists, the matter may have to be decided by the appropriate court.

It is extremely important for the trustee to be given adequate powers under the trust instruments. While the powers authorized under state law may be substantial, they are never as complete as those which can be provided in the instrument itself.

FEATURES ATTRIBUTABLE TO BOTH INTERVIVOS AND TESTAMENTARY TRUSTS

Avoidance of Multiple Taxation of the Same Assets—Any assets you leave outright to a beneficiary are going to be taxed in your estate and also in the beneficiary's estate. The only exception to this is the Marital Deduction which enables a married person to transfer the greater of 50% of the adjusted gross estate or $250,000 to the surviving spouse free of estate tax. The following examples will illustrate how taxes can be saved through the use of trusts.

Example 1—Perry Wise has an estate of $500,000 which he plans to leave outright to his wife, Penny. Penny's will then leaves the entire estate to their two children. Upon Perry's death, the estate would be subject to $23,800 in federal estate taxes. Then upon Penny's subsequent death the taxes would be $100,-700. This would result in the children receiving $375,500. If Perry creates a marital deduction trust, Penny can still receive the income from all the property, but the tax consequences would change dramatically. Upon Perry's death, the taxes would still be $23,800, but upon Penny's subsequent death they would only be $23,800 resulting in savings for the children of $76,900.

Example 2—Joe Solo is a bachelor. In the event of his death, he wants his sister, Susie, to receive everything he has. If Susie doesn't survive him, his estate is to go to her children. Joe has an estate of $300,000. If we assume Joe's sister has no assets of her own, the federal estate tax on Joe's death will be $40,800, and on Susie's death the tax will be $26,900. If Joe leaves the estate in trust giving Susie the income for life and providing that the principal go to the children, the only tax would be the $40,800 payable upon Joe's death. No tax would be payable upon Susie's subsequent death, resulting in savings of $26,900.

INVESTMENT MANAGEMENT

If your beneficiaries have never made investment decisions, the moment of your death may not be the time to burden them with those responsibilities. A trust places the responsibility for keeping the estate productive on the shoulders of your trustee. Without a trust your beneficiaries will be forced to assume the burden of investment management. If everything is left outright to your spouse and she has small children at home, she would probably have her hands full trying to raise them and be unable to devote adequate time to investment management. If your beneficiaries are young adults, they might not yet be financially mature enough to make responsible investment decisions.

Rather than requiring your heirs to manage their own investments before they are prepared to do so, you might use a professional trustee and have that trustee consult with them to make them aware of why the various investment decisions are being made. This will provide them with excellent training for that point when they will be forced to assume those responsibilities.

PROTECTION FROM THEMSELVES AND OTHERS

We all hear of cases in which financial scavengers and piranha-like relatives take advantage of widows, widowers, and youthful heirs. Sometimes it's the brother-in-law who has a business idea that will make them both wealthy. Or it might be a "financial advisor" who has a unique opportunity in Alaskan condominiums, or it might be a child who has an opportunity to get in on the ground floor of a company making steam-driven automobiles. Trusts can protect against this type of problem by resting total investment responsibility in an independent trustee.

It is also often important to protect beneficiaries against themselves. Several years ago, a young California woman inherited over $200,000 from her father. She and her family spent a year traveling all over the world and at the end of that year were not only broke but heavily in debt. When asked whether she regretted what she had done, she replied that she had no regrets and if given the opportunity would do exactly the same thing again. When I think of this story I can't help but wonder whether her father, who worked so hard to accumulate that money, is resting comfortably or turning over and over in his grave. A trust can protect against this type of imprudence.

KEEPING ASSETS IN THE FAMILY

Childless couples often feel trusts are unnecessary for them; however, many ignore a serious problem which occurs time and again. I recall one couple who executed identical wills leaving everything outright to the survivor and then providing that upon the survivor's death one-half would go to the husband's brother and the other one-half would be divided equally among the wife's brothers and sisters. The husband died first and immediately after his death his widow changed her will. She cut out her brother-in-law, claiming her family needed the money more than he did. While her reasoning might have been correct, it was contrary to her husband's desires. The husband's side of the family would have been protected if he had placed one-half of the assets in trust with the income payable to his wife and the principal to his brother.

Another fairly common occurrence is the one in which a married couple with children have all their assets in joint tenancy. Sometimes after one spouse (A) dies, the surviving spouse (B) remarries. In order to show affection and trust for the new spouse (C), the assets are once again put into joint tenancy. Upon the surviving spouse's (B) death, the children of the first marriage are effectively disinherited because all of the assets go to the new spouse as a result of joint tenancy. This problem can also be corrected through the use of a trust. The first spouse (A) could leave part of the property in trust for the survivor with the remainder going to the children. The surviving spouse would enjoy the benefits for life but could not intentionally or unintentionally divert the principal from the children.

FLEXIBILITY

A trust can be designed to provide for almost any occasion that might arise. Its flexibility depends upon the amount of discretion you decide to give to your trustee. For example, rather than requiring distribution of income to specific beneficiaries, you can give the trustee discretion to pay income to various beneficiaries in whatever proportions he deems advisable. You might want to provide for a son and his family. If that son is currently in a high income tax bracket, the trustee could distribute income to or for the benefit of the son's children and it would be taxable in their brackets. On the other hand, if your son falls on hard times, the income can be made available to him.

Powers of appointment add to the flexibility of trusts. The income beneficiary, for example, could be given a power of appointment enabling him to change distribution among the remaindermen. If one of the remaindermen becomes an alcoholic or spendthrift, his share of the estate can be restricted through exercise of the power of appointment.

Income beneficiaries can be given the right to withdraw principal on their own volition without requiring approval of the trustee. If the right of withdrawal is restricted to the greater of $5,000 or 5% of the principal, that principal avoids inclusion in the beneficiary's estate.

These are but a few of the examples of flexibility involved in the use of trusts.

AVOIDANCE OF GUARDIANSHIP AND ABILITY TO WITHHOLD DISTRIBUTIONS FOR MINORS

If a minor inherits property it is usually held in a guardianship for him until he attains majority, at which time it is distributed outright. This poses two problems. First, guardianship, in most instances, is a cumbersome and costly process. Court approval is usually required before any distributions can be made for the child's benefit. Second, eighteen is the age of majority in many states and twenty-one in the rest. Most children at those ages are not yet financially mature enough to handle substantial amounts of money.

Trusts can avoid both of these problems. The trustee can be given discretion to use whatever amounts it deems necessary to provide for the minor's needs. The children can be well taken care of without continuously obtaining court approval. Many settlors ask how difficult it is for the guardian of the person to obtain funds from a trustee. If the trustee is acting responsibly, the guardian should have no difficulty whatsoever in obtaining the amounts he needs to provide adequately for the minor.

Distributions of principal (the assets of the trust) can be withheld until the child is old enough to fully appreciate the value of a dollar. You can also stagger distributions so that the child will not receive his entire inheritance at one time. If he dissipates his first distribution, he will have time to think about his mistakes before the next distribution is made.

Some trusts give the trustee absolute discretion over principal distributions. The purpose is to guarantee that the child is capable of handling money before any principal distributions are made outright to him. This is a tremendous responsibility to place upon a trustee. In order to fulfill that responsibility he must be completely honest and capable of exercising discretion impartially.

CONCLUSION

This chapter has discussed the attributes of trusts in general. It has explained what a trust is, identified the parties to a trust, suggested what to look for in a trustee, defined the powers and duties of a trustee, and discussed some of the advantages attributable to both intervivos and testamentary trusts. You begin to get an idea of how trusts can be used in your estate plan. In the next two chapters, you will gain an appreciation for the revocable and irrevocable living trust.

CHAPTER X

THE REVOCABLE LIVING TRUST

The revocable living trust, as defined in the preceding chapter, is one which comes into existence during the settlor's lifetime and over which he has the power to amend, revoke, activate, or deactivate at any time. This trust can be extremely valuable if properly used.

THE PASSIVE LIVING TRUST (THE LIFE INSURANCE TRUST)

A living trust which contains no assets is called a passive trust. The most common form of passive trust is usually referred to as the life insurance trust because the only property interest it contains is a beneficial interest in the settlor's life insurance policies. That is, the trustor has named his trustee as beneficiary of his life insurance policies.

This form of trust is usually substituted for a testamentary trust. Many attorneys prefer it because it avoids the necessity for court supervision; however, this is no longer a significant advantage in those states whose laws provide for unsupervised administration. Another reason why life insurance trusts are favored is that the trustee does not have to wait for court appointment to collect the insurance proceeds. Once again, most states have simplified their probate procedures to enable a testamentary trustee to be appointed quickly in order for him to make claim against the insurance companies.

Another distinction between a testamentary trust and a living trust is that the will creating the testamentary trust must be administered in the testator's state of residence. If the testator moves, his testamentary trustee may not be able to act in the new state. On the other hand, if he has a living trust, it can continue to be administered by the trustee of his choice and his will can distribute assets to that trust regardless of where he lives.

The passive trust can be funded at any time. If the settlor knows he has only a short time to live, he can place his assets in the trust and thereby avoid the costs and delays of probate. As you will see later, there may be other factors making it inadvisable to avoid probate.

THE ACTIVE LIVING TRUST

An active living trust is one which you fund during your lifetime. It also can substitute for the testamentary trust; however, there are many which terminate on the settlor's death and distribute to his estate. There are a great many reasons why this type of trust is created. We will describe some of those reasons; however, the reasons are so many and varied it would be beyond the scope of this book to discuss them all.

SEGREGATING ASSETS

Some people create living trusts in order to keep certain assets separate from others. For example, a widow who is contemplating remarriage might place all of her assets in a living trust with her children as ultimate beneficiaries in order to keep from commingling them with her new husband's assets. A couple moving from a community property state to a non-community property state may place their community assets in trust to maintain their identity as community property.

PROPERTY MANAGEMENT

Many businessmen do not have the time or inclination to manage their own investments. Others have found the decisions they make are based more on emotion than on facts and consequently have suffered losses managing their own investments. These people recognize the value of professional management and are willing to turn those responsibilities over to a corporate trustee.

Many younger widows create living trusts both for management and to protect the assets from financial scavengers. They recognize the need for management and their susceptibility to people who appear to be interested in them emotionally.

Another group who crave management are the elderly. During retirement they may not want to be saddled with the burdens of management. They want to be free to travel and enjoy life. Management and protection from incapacity motivate many elderly people to create living trusts.

PROTECTION FROM PHYSICAL OR MENTAL INCAPACITY

Many elderly people see their friends becoming senile or physically disabled. They recognize it could happen to them at any time and rather than risk the possible loss of assets through mismanagement or coercion they create living trusts. The alternative is a guardianship or conservatorship and most are not willing to suggest they might be incompetent or unable to handle their own affairs. No such admission is made when they create a living trust. On the contrary, they have to be competent to execute a trust.

There are other factors involved in choosing between a trust and a conservatorship. The trust is usually less expensive, because it is not necessary to account to the court or obtain court approval for expenditures or investment changes. The trust is also more flexible in that the trustee's powers as specified in the trust instrument are usually much broader than would be allowed in a conservatorship.

PRIVACY

In most states probate records are public records. Anyone can have access to them. Trust records are private, available only to the beneficiaries themselves. Mayor Richard Daley of Chicago, who died in 1977, had placed most of his assets in a living trust; consequently it was impossible for the press to obtain much information concerning his estate.

Some people are interested in privacy during their lifetimes as well. They will create trusts placing their assets in the trustee's name, but retain the right to direct investments. This enables them to accumulate property in complete anonymity.

AVOIDANCE OF COSTS AND DELAYS OF PROBATE

In most states, assets in a living trust will avoid probate. The primary advantage in avoiding probate is not cost saving, but, rather, convenience. Probate can be a slow and cumbersome process. There are, however, many advantages of probate which should be given consideration. First, notice to creditors must be published in order to protect the estate from future claims. This can be done by the trustee, but it is an integral part of the probate process. Second, the probate estate provides opportunities for income tax savings through the manipulation of fiscal years. If there are both a living trust and a probate estate, several short fiscal years can be obtained, thereby reducing income taxes significantly. Finally, the costs incurred in managing a living trust during the settlor's lifetime must be considered.

REDUCE POSSIBILITY OF CONTEST

A will or a living trust can be attacked on the grounds of undue influence or the testator's lack of mental capacity; however, such an attack is far less likely to succeed against a living trust which has been in existence for several years. From time to time one spouse will create a living trust in an attempt to prevent the other spouse from claiming a statutory right in the property. Apparently, there are some jurisdictions in which this can be done; however, it appears the majority of states would hold in favor of the surviving spouse.

OBSERVE THE TRUSTEE IN ACTION

Some people create living trusts so they can observe how the trustee will handle their affairs after they are gone. This is usually accomplished by placing part or all of the assets in trust and reserving the right to be consulted by the trustee concerning investment changes. This enables him to both observe how the trustee operates and become aware of the factors the trustee believes are important in decision making.

TAX IMPLICATIONS OF THE REVOCABLE LIVING TRUST

The income from a revocable living trust is taxable to the settlor for federal income tax purposes. Some states may impose either an income tax and/or a personal property tax on the trust. Even though the trust itself does not pay a federal income tax, the trustee should obtain a taxpayer identification number and file an initial fiduciary information return. Some attorneys recommend that such returns be filed each year to avoid any question of the trust's validity.

After the settlor's death, the trustee can select whatever fiscal year it deems advisable for the trust. The selection of fiscal years should be coordinated with the executor of the estate and any surviving spouse.

Potential federal estate tax savings were discussed in the prior chapter. Suffice it to say here that no tax savings occur upon the settlor's death, unless there are charitable beneficiaries. All assets in the revocable living trust are includible in his gross estate.

CONCLUSION

The passive living trust is a commonly used substitute for a testamentary trust. It is primarily a receptacle for life insurance proceeds. The active trust has a great many lifetime uses such as management, protection against physical or mental incapacity, privacy, and the opportunity to observe the trustee in action. They are both extremely useful tools and should be considered as possible vehicles to use in most estate plans. The irrevocable trusts discussed in the next chapter are designed to accomplish specific individual objectives and not as commonly used as the revocable living trusts.

CHAPTER XI

THE IRREVOCABLE LIVING TRUST

Irrevocable living trusts are normally created for tax purposes; however, from time to time individuals will create such trusts for other reasons. No one should establish an irrevocable trust if it is likely he might need the assets in the near future or if it is possible his objectives might change.

REASONS FOR CREATING IRREVOCABLE TRUSTS

The Settlor Creates a Trust to Protect Himself—You would think anyone who is intelligent enough to recognize his limitations would also be smart enough to manage his own affairs; however, this is not always the case. A young man might inherit a substantial amount of money and recognize that he does not yet have the maturity to manage it, or a young widow may want to be certain no man will marry her for her money. The irrevocable trust accomplishes these objectives by restricting the settlor to the income unless emergencies arise, under which circumstances the trustee can use the principal for the settlor's benefit.

The Trust Is Created to Make a Family Member Financially Independent—A dependent parent may feel uncomfortable taking a check directly from a child. Placing assets in trust for that parent may give him or her a feeling of independence. Even though the support is coming from the same source, there is often a psychological difference. A daughter may marry a man who is unable to support her in the style to which she has become accustomed or a son may have an impairment that makes it difficult for him to earn a reasonable living. An irrevocable trust can once again provide them with an independent source of income so there is no longer any necessity to ask their parents for money.

Protection Against Potential Creditors—An irrevocable trust which is created for the sole purpose of defrauding creditors can be set aside; however, if the trust is established prior to incurring obligations, it should conserve the assets. For example, if an individual considers undertaking a hazardous business venture, he might place the majority of his personal assets in trust in order to safeguard them for his family.

Tax Consequences of Irrevocable Trusts—The income from irrevocable trusts is taxable to the beneficiary if the trust has a duration of more than ten years and the trustor retains no elements of control over the trust. If the income is used to provide items for the beneficiary which would constitute support for which the settlor is legally responsible, the income will be taxed to the trustor. For example, if the income is used to provide for the education of a child, the funds used to provide that education will be taxable to the settlor. If the income is used to pay premiums for life insurance on the settlor's life, the income will be taxable to the settlor. Great care needs to be taken in drafting an irrevocable trust to assure the income will not be taxable to the settlor. Irrevocable trusts created prior to the 1976 Tax Reform Act would escape estate taxation if properly drafted and if the settlor retained no rights. Such trusts created today will only escape estate taxation to the extent contributions to the trust fall within the available annual exclusions. For example, if there are three beneficiaries of an irrevocable trust, up to $9,000 ($3,000 per beneficiary) of the funds added to that trust each year can avoid taxation in the settlor's estate.

TYPES OF IRREVOCABLE TRUSTS

The Ten-year Reversionary Trust—If assets are placed in trust for a period of more than ten years, the income is taxable to the beneficiary. The present value of the income is treated as a gift to the beneficiary subject only to the $3,000 annual exclusion. For example, if A places $50,000 in trust for a period of ten years and one day, naming his three children as beneficiaries, and that trust generates $3,900 per year of income to the children, it will have the following consequences:

1. $3,900 of income will be taxable to the three children in their relatively low tax brackets. The amount of annual tax savings would depend upon the settlor's tax bracket.
2. $22,500 will be treated as a gift from A to his children. $9,000 will qualify for the annual exclusion and $13,500 will be subject to the unified transfer tax. ($18,000 would be excluded if the wife joins in the gift.)

Ten-year reversionary trusts are used primarily to transfer income into lower tax brackets; however, they can accomplish other important objectives. They provide an economical way for the settlor to contribute to the support of an elderly parent. They also enable a parent to provide extra income to his children using pre-tax dollars.

Irrevocable Trusts for Minors—If a trust is created for the benefit of a minor which requires the trustee to distribute corpus and accumulated income at age twenty-one, the full value of the property transferred will qualify for the annual exclusion. This enables a parent or grandparent to transfer $3,000 per year in trust for each child or grandchild. If the spouse joins in these gifts $6,000 per year can be set aside for each beneficiary. The same benefits can be obtained without requiring distributions to the beneficiary at age twenty-one if the beneficiary has the right to request distribution.

Lifetime Irrevocable Trusts—Many settlors are interested in providing a lifetime income for certain beneficiaries. If this is done through the medium of an irrevocable trust, the present value of the income he can anticipate receiving will qualify for the annual exclusion. Assume a trust is created for a twenty-three-year-old man to which the settlor and his wife contribute $6,500. The factor representing the present value of his income is .90292. This means $5,868.98 will be excluded from taxation and $631.02 will be subject to the unified transfer tax.

STATE GIFT TAXES

While it is possible for fairly substantial gifts to be made in trust without incurring an immediate federal tax, there might be some state taxes due. It is imperative that the tax consequences be analyzed carefully by a competent CPA or tax attorney.

THE IRREVOCABLE LIFE INSURANCE TRUST

The irrevocable life insurance trust should be given consideration in planning for substantial estates. The primary purpose of this trust is avoidance of death taxes through the transfer of all incidences of ownership in insurance policies from the insured to a trustee. A properly drawn, carefully implemented trust can avoid taxation of life insurance policies on the deaths of both the husband and the wife.

The estate tax consequences under three different plans will illustrate the value of this type of trust. In the first plan we will assume the insurance is owned by the insured and included in his estate. In the second, we will assume it is owned by his wife and not includible in his estate, but includible in the wife's estate upon her subsequent death. In the third situation, we will assume it is owned by the trust and not includible in either estate. In each of the three situations, the will provides for a marital deduction trust designed to minimize taxes over both deaths. Our hypothetical decedent has tangible taxable assets totaling $500,000 and $200,000 of life insurance.

Plan I—Insurance owned by the decedent		
Fed. taxes on husband's death	$57,800	
Fed. taxes on wife's death	57,800	
Total taxes on both deaths		$115,600
Plan II—Insurance owned by the wife		
Fed. taxes on husband's death	23,800	
Fed. taxes on wife's death	91,800	
Total taxes on both deaths		$115,600
Plan III—Insurance owned by the trust		
Fed. taxes on husband's death	$23,800	
Fed. taxes on wife's death	23,800	
Total taxes on both deaths		$47,600

As you can see overall taxes in this estate would be reduced $68,000 by the use of the irrevocable life insurance trust. The savings become more dramatic as the estate increases in size.

Flexibility is limited with any irrevocable trust; consequently this type of trust should only be used if it accomplishes some of your primary objectives over and above tax savings. One objective that can be accomplished is to provide cash to pay estate settlement costs. You cannot require the trustee to pay those costs or the proceeds will be taxable; however, you can give the trustee the right to lend money to or buy assets from the estate. In this way, cash can be made available to the estate without forcing the liquidation of assets.

Another objective this trust can accomplish is the generation of income for family members. The assets purchased from the estate or the loan to the estate will produce income which can be paid out to the beneficiaries. Your spouse, children, or any other person could be income beneficiaries.

There are several possible disadvantages to the irrevocable life insurance trust. In order to qualify the annual premium payments as gifts of a present interest for purposes of the $3,000 annual exclusion, most authorities suggest the beneficiaries be given certain immediate rights. They should probably have a non-cumulative annual right of withdrawal equivalent to the lesser of the amount of premiums paid or $5,000. This right could probably terminate at your death since you would no longer be interested in obtaining the annual gift tax exclusion. It is highly unlikely any child, particularly a minor, will exercise the right of withdrawal, but if you don't provide for it, all premiums and possibly the insurance proceeds themselves will be included in your estate.

Another disadvantage is the lack of flexibility. If your objectives change, you cannot change the trust. For example, if a son or daughter does something which displeases you, the trust cannot be changed to omit that child. One possible answer is to give your spouse a limited power of appointment to change distribution among your children and grandchildren, or your trustee could be given the right to terminate the trust and distribute to the beneficiaries if it feels the trust is no longer serving a useful purpose. Upon such distribution you could buy back the policies for their current cash value and the trustee could distribute cash to the beneficiaries.

Another problem arises if your spouse is a beneficiary of the trust and you become divorced—that spouse will still be a beneficiary. In order to avoid this problem, the trust instrument could define "spouse" as meaning the person who at the time of your death is your spouse. This type of definition might create some friction between you and your spouse if that spouse is not understanding or receptive.

You might apply for a substantial loan on which your banker wants an assignment of an insurance policy. You will have absolutely no ability to assign an interest in any policy held as an asset of your trust.

In order to assure that the IRS will treat the trust as being a true transfer of ownership in the policies, it would be advisable to use an independent trustee who is not subservient to you in any way. The safest approach is to name a corporate fiduciary. They will probably charge a small annual fee because of the responsibilities involved in handling irrevocable trusts; however, assurance the plan will work may be worth the expense.

TAX CONSEQUENCES

Gift Taxes—A gift takes place upon the transfer of an existing policy into the trust. The value of a paid-up policy would be its replacement cost. The value of a policy on which you have been paying premiums for some time would be its interpolated terminal reserve. (This approximates the policy's cash values.) A new policy with no cash values would probably be valued based on the unused premium. An individual who is currently uninsurable might have a difficult time justifying any value other than the face value of the contract; however, the attorney might feel it is worth the chance to try valuing policies based on standard approaches. If the transfer qualifies as a gift of a present interest, you will be allowed an exclusion of $3,000 multiplied by the number of beneficiaries who have non-cumulative rights of withdrawal. Amounts over and above the annual exclusion would be treated as future interest gifts and taxable subject to the unified tax credit. Subsequent premium payments up to $3,000 per beneficiary should also qualify as present interest gifts. Your spouse could join in the gifts, thereby increasing the excludible amount to $6,000 per beneficiary; however, this poses two potential problems. If the spouse is also an income beneficiary, the portion of the trust attributable to her gift would be included in her estate. Whether she is a beneficiary or not, her share of the three years' premiums paid prior to her husband's death would be included in his estate.

Income Taxes—If the trust is funded with income producing assets and the trustee has authority to use that income to pay premiums, the income so used will be taxable to the grantor. If any income is payable to the beneficiaries it will be taxable to them.

Estate Taxes—It appears the proceeds will escape estate taxation if the insured survives the transfer of the policies by at least three years. If he dies within three years, the proceeds are likely to be taxed in his estate. The Internal Revenue Service consistently attempts to include insurance proceeds in the taxable estate regardless of ownership, but if the trust is properly drawn and the insured retains no elements of control whatsoever, the proceeds should escape taxation.

CONCLUSION

The irrevocable life insurance trust is valuable in planning for relatively large estates. An individual whose family is grown and who has a stable marriage should seriously consider using it in his estate plan. Younger or less stable people should probably consider other alternatives because of the limited flexibility.

CHAPTER XII

LIFE INSURANCE

Life insurance is not only a valuable asset in your estate, but it is also one of the most useful tools available to the estate planner. The individual who has enough foresight to acquire substantial amounts of life insurance at an early age will have most of his estate planning problems solved before they become problems.

PURPOSES OF LIFE INSURANCE

Life insurance serves three primary purposes in the average estate plan. First, it assures your family of adequate food, clothing, and shelter in the event of your death. Hopefully, you can afford enough life insurance so they can continue to maintain the standard of living you are currently providing for them.

The second purpose of life insurance is to provide you with supplementary retirement income if your other sources are inadequate. This purpose can only be accomplished with cash value life insurance and not term insurance.

The third purpose of life insurance is to provide ready liquidity in your estate to make certain your estate settlement costs can be paid without forcing the sale of other assets at what might be the wrong time. If you wait to buy life insurance until your potential estate settlement costs are relatively high, you may find the cost prohibitive or the coverage unavailable to you.

There are many other uses of life insurance such as funding buy-sell agreements and making charitable gifts, but the above three uses are the most prevalent in estate planning.

HOW MUCH LIFE INSURANCE DO YOU NEED?

The amount of life insurance an individual needs is a perpetual question to which there is no one answer. Each person must make his own determination based on his own circumstances; however, there are a few basic concepts and guidelines of which you should be aware.

Insurance to Provide Family Income—Two approaches currently being used by the insurance industry are programming and capital needs analysis. Programming consists of charting the amount of income your spouse and children can anticipate receiving from social security, veterans' benefits, your personal assets, and other sources, and then determining, by the use of various settlement options, how much insurance is needed using both interest and principal to create the required additional income. Agents using the capital needs approach total the amount of money required to pay estate settlement costs, provide college educations, and meet other fixed obligations and add to that figure the amount of principal necessary to provide a specified income assuming a specified rate of return.

Example: Assume Mr. Jones wants to provide $30,000 for his children's education, $40,000 to pay off his mortgage, and $10,000 to meet estate settlement costs. In addition, he wants to provide his wife with an income of $1,000 per month. He believes a conservative return on capital would be 6%; consequently the amount of capital required to produce

$1,000 per month would be $200,000 ($12,000 ÷ .06). His total capital need would be $280,000.

This illustration is oversimplified because it ignores other assets and income available from social security; however, it does illustrate the basic concept of capital needs analysis.

A new objective approach to calculating family income needs was developed by First National City Bank. Their economists and insurance experts analyzed the finances of a family of four and determined that family could maintain a decent standard of living with an after tax income of 60 to 75% of the breadwinner's after tax income. The bank then developed a multiples-of-salary chart which reflects social security, projects a 5% rate of return, and assumes principal would be used over the surviving spouse's lifetime. In determining the total amount required, the amount calculated from the chart needs to be reduced by the amount of liquid assets in excess of one year's gross income. If liquid assets are less than one year's gross income, the insurance need should be increased by the amount necessary to provide an additional one year's gross income.

Example: Mr. and Mrs. C. Cure have a gross income of $23,500 per year. They currently own a house, car, miscellaneous personal property, and $10,000 in a bank account. Mrs. Cure is thirty-five years old. Using the following table, we see that Mr. Cure should have life insurance totaling between 5.5 and eight times his current income or from $129,250 to $188,000. Add to this amount the $13,500 ($23,-500 minus $10,000) necessary to provide liquid assets equivalent to one year's income, and the amount required will fall between $142,750 and $201,500, depending on whether the family will be maintained at the 60 or 75% level.

MULTIPLES-OF-SALARY CHART

Breadwinner's Gross earnings	Present Age of Spouse							
	25		35		45		55	
	75%	60%	75%	60%	75%	60%	75%	60%
$ 9,000	4.0	3.0	5.5	4.0	7.5	5.5	6.5	4.5
15,000	4.5	3.0	6.5	4.5	8.0	6.0	7.0	5.5
24,000	6.5	4.5	8.0	5.5	8.5	6.5	7.5	5.5
30,000	7.5	5.0	8.0	6.0	8.5	6.5	7.0	5.5
40,000	7.5	5.0	8.0	6.0	8.0	6.0	7.0	5.5
65,000	7.5	5.5	7.5	6.0	7.5	6.0	6.5	5.0

The Citibank approach provides as good a guideline as possible, but it, like the programming approach and capital needs analysis, ignores inflation. Many insurance men attempt to compensate for inflation in one or both of two ways. First, they increase the face amount based on what you feel the inflation rate will be, and second, they provide for payment in a lump sum to provide the beneficiaries greater investment flexibility. Another possibility is the relatively new concept "adjustable life." This is a policy which allows the acquisition of additional amounts of insurance approximating increases in the cost of living, without evidence of insurability.

I often hear the statement, "If anything happens to me, my wife can go back to work," or, "My wife will remarry." There are several reasons why these assumptions are dangerous. If a widow with minor children returns to work, she will lose a substantial part of her social security benefits. If she waits until the children are grown to return to work, she may have difficulty entering the job market due to age or lack of experience. It might be healthy for a widow to go to work, but it doesn't make sense to force her to take some sort of menial job you wouldn't condone if you were still here.

The second argument relating to a widow remarrying is one I hope comes true, because most people need the companionship that accompanies marriage; however, the facts of the matter are the majority of widows over forty do not remarry. And it is not always easy for a younger widow to find a desirable man willing to assume responsibility for several small children.

INSURANCE FOR ESTATE LIQUIDITY

If the primary purpose for your insurance is to provide liquid assets with which to pay your estate settlement costs, you need a fairly accurate assessment of what those costs are going to be. Your attorney, CPA, or trust officer can give you a fairly accurate estimate based on your assets as they are today;

however, circumstances change. Revisions in the tax law can increase or decrease your tax liability. Changes in your estate plan can result in higher or lower costs. Your investment or business management abilities may substantially increase your estate. These factors and others must be taken into consideration in determining how much insurance you need for estate settlement costs.

The minimum amount of insurance you need if you want to protect your assets for your heirs is an amount adequate to cover the estate settlement costs based on your estate as it stands today. The maximum amount will depend on how large you expect your estate to be in the future.

The following table approximates what might be required to cover average taxes, probate costs, and other expenses in estates of various sizes. These are approximations only, based on California probate and inheritance taxes. The costs in your estate could vary significantly from these estimates.

Size of Estate	Total Cash Needs	
	Spouse Survives	No Spouse Survives
$ 100,000	$ 7,000	$ 9,500
120,000	8,300	11,400
140,000	10,000	13,400
150,000	10,600	15,200
170,000	11,700	17,300
190,000	13,300	19,300
200,000	14,200	23,400
220,000	15,500	31,700
240,000	17,100	40,300
260,000	18,700	48,900
280,000	20,000	57,500
300,000	21,300	66,100
320,000	23,100	74,700
340,000	24,900	85,300
360,000	26,700	93,900
380,000	28,500	103,500
400,000	33,300	113,100

420,000	38,100	123,100
440,000	42,900	133,100
460,000	48,700	143,100
480,000	53,700	153,100
500,000	58,700	163,100
600,000	82,700	209,100
700,000	106,700	257,100
800,000	130,700	305,100
900,000	154,700	355,100
1,000,000	178,700	405,100

TERM VS. PERMANENT INSURANCE

What type of life insurance should you acquire? All life insurance falls into two basic categories: term insurance and permanent insurance. Each has many variations.

Term Insurance—Term insurance is the simplest form of life insurance. You pay the insurance company premiums for a specific period of time and it agrees to pay your beneficiary a certain benefit if your death occurs during that time. There are no cash buildups in the policy, and each time the policy is renewed the rates increase. The premiums for term insurance at any age are less than the premiums for permanent insurance at the same age. Most companies will not issue term insurance after age sixty-five. Anyone who anticipates an insurance need that will extend beyond age sixty-five—such as insurance for estate liquidity—should definitely acquire permanent insurance.

The two most common types of term insurance are *level term* and *decreasing term.* Level term provides level coverage for a fixed period of time. The most common level term periods are one year and five years. At the end of the term period, the premium increases if you want to maintain the same coverage. Decreasing term insurance provides benefits which reduce each year during the period of benefit while the premium remains constant. Term insurance should be *renewable* and *convertible.* A renewable provision in a policy guarantees that you can renew the policy at the end of the term period. If the policy contains a conversion right, it means you can convert to some form of permanent insurance before the end of the term period. Both of these provisions are important because they assure you of being able to obtain insurance even though you may no longer be insurable.

Permanent Insurance—Permanent insurance is also known as whole life or ordinary life insurance. While term policies expire at some future date, permanent policies remain in force as long as the insured lives and pays the premiums. You normally pay premiums on an ordinary life policy for as long as you live if you want to maintain full coverage. A variation on the ordinary life policy is called limited pay life. You agree to pay premiums for a fixed number of years—ten, twenty, or to age sixty-five—and the insurance remains in force for your lifetime. The premiums are higher than for ordinary life because you pay for a much shorter period of time. Another variation on the ordinary life policy is called an endowment contract. You might pay $1,000 each year for ten years on a $10,000 ten-year endowment contract. If you die at any time during that ten-year period, your family receives $10,000. If you live the full ten-year period, you receive $10,000.

Nonforfeiture Values—All permanent policies contain three basic "non-forfeiture values": cash values, extended term, and paid-up insurance. Each year part of your premium goes into a reserve account. You can borrow up to 95% of that reserve account at any time or you can terminate the policy and withdraw the entire cash value.

The extended term privilege enables you to discontinue paying premiums and allow your cash values to keep the full face amount of insurance in force for a fixed period of time.

> **Example:** A man age forty buys a $25,000 policy and pays on it for ten years at which time he decides to discontinue paying premiums. At that time he has

cash values of $5,000. If he elects to take extended term, the full $25,000 will remain in force for twelve years.

The cash values can also be used to buy paid-up coverage at an amount less than the face value which will remain in force for the remainder of your life. Under this alternative, you continue to have access to the cash values of the policy.

Example: If the man in the previous example elects to take paid-up insurance instead of extended term, $10,000 of coverage would remain in force for his lifetime. In addition, the $5,000 cash value would be available to him if he ever needs it.

Term for Temporary Needs and Permanent for Permanent Needs—Term insurance should be used only to cover temporary needs or to guarantee your insurability until you can afford the increased premium necessary to acquire permanent insurance. Some examples of temporary needs might be debt repayment, educational funds, and so forth. Permanent insurance should be used to cover such needs as estate settlement costs and continuing income for your spouse. The net cost of permanent insurance over several years will usually be less than the cost of term insurance; consequently permanent insurance is often used to satisfy temporary needs.

The following table illustrates the lower net cost of permanent insurance. You will notice that the net premium for permanent is less than the term premium in the third year and the permanent policy begins to show a profit in the eighth year. This illustration ignores the earning ability of the difference between the term and permanent premiums, but as you will see in a subsequent example relating to "Buy Term and Invest the Difference," that ability is of little advantage.

10-YEAR COMPARISON OF TERM VERSUS PERMANENT PREMIUM*

YEAR	PERMANENT PREMIUM	-LESS-	DIVIDEND	-LESS-	CASH VALUE INCREASE	=	NET COST	TERM PREMIUM	ANNUAL DIFFERENCE	CUMULATIVE PROFIT FROM PERMANENT
1	2986	—	–0–	—	–0–	=	(2986)	−517	2469	(2469)
2	2986	—	–0–	—	2200	=	(786)	−572	214	(2673)
3	2986	—	180	—	2580	=	(226)	−589	−363	(2310)
4	2986	—	263	—	2383	=	(340)	−627	−287	(2023)
5	2986	—	345	—	2482	=	(159)	−669	−510	(1513)
6	2986	—	429	—	2584	=	27	−710	−737	(776)
7	2986	—	513	—	2484	=	11	−757	−768	(8)
8	2986	—	597	—	2584	=	195	−803	−998	990
9	2986	—	681	—	2584	=	279	−851	−1130	2120
10	2986	—	765	—	2584	=	363	−910	−1273	3393

**This table reflects a major company's rates for $100,000 policies for a male age forty-five in 1974.*

Stock vs. Mutual Companies (Participating vs. Non-Participating Policies)—There are two basic types of insurance companies: mutual companies and stock companies. Mutual companies are owned by the policyholders while stock companies are owned by the stockholders who may or may not also be policyholders. Mutual companies issue what are known as "participating" policies. What this means is that policyholders participate in the profits of the company through premium refunds (dividends). These dividends usually result from operating efficiencies and better than projected investment returns. Dividends cannot be accurately determined in advance; however, most good companies have continually paid out more in dividends than was actually projected. Stock companies usually issue non-participating policies, and their profits are passed on to the stockholders instead of the policyholders. Some also issue participating policies in which the policyholders can share. You might ask why anyone would buy a non-participating policy. The initial premiums on non-participating policies are approximately 30% less than the initial premiums for participating policies. These premiums will remain constant for the life of the policy. The dividends on participating policies may ultimately reduce the net premium on those policies below those of non-participating policies; however, there is no guarantee. Many purchasers prefer to buy a policy on which they know exactly what the premium is going to be for the rest of their lives rather than pay a higher premium today in anticipation of lower premiums in the future.

Net Cost—We have referred to net cost several times. What is net cost and how is it calculated? Net cost is the cost to you of pure protection after separating out cash values and dividends. True net cost for non-participating policies is relatively easy to ascertain because the premiums and cash values are fixed and there are no dividends to take into consideration. Premiums on participating policies must be adjusted to reflect projected dividends. Inasmuch as those dividends might increase or decrease, the net cost calculations at the time the policy is purchased may be inaccurate.

The majority of the industry now accepts the "interest adjusted method" for determining net cost. This is a formula which takes into consideration the time value of money. It applies an interest rate to the premiums to reflect what your money could have earned if it were invested elsewhere. The result is a factor which approximates the time value for each thousand dollars of coverage. Obviously, this is not an exact science and the true net cost of any policy depends upon when and how it is terminated. For example, the net cost for a policy which is surrendered would be greater than one on which a death claim is paid.

Bests Flitcraft, which rates most good companies, reflects the interest adjusted method in its comparison of various policies. Theoretically, the lower the factor the better the policy, but Bests cautions that the interest adjusted index is just an index and nothing more. Next time you are considering a life insurance purchase, ask to see how the company rates in Bests, but don't base your purchase entirely on their rating. Your agent and the quality of service he provides for you should be given equal consideration.

Buy Term and Invest the Difference—For many years now, a multitude of financial planners have advocated the "buy term and invest the difference" concept. The people recommending this approach suggest you are imprudent leaving your money with the insurance company. Term insurance will provide the same death benefit and you can use your excess cash for other investments. This concept got its start during the sixties (the heyday of mutual funds) when mutual fund salesmen were selling both term insurance and funds. Many people who accepted the concept at that time ended up with far less than they would have had by buying permanent life insurance, some because they lost on their investments and others because they failed to save and invest the difference.

Some years ago, M. Albert Linton, the chairman of the board of Provident Mutual Life Insurance Company and former president of the Actuarial Society of America, made a study of the investment attributes of whole life insurance. Mr. Linton's study, which was computer generated, compared the investment value of a whole life policy to a renewable term policy, with the difference in premiums devoted to separate investments. The results were surprising!

To obtain a return from separate investments equivalent to what could be obtained from a whole life policy over a twenty-year period, the investor would have to earn a net return, after taxes and expenses, of 4.78%. This is the equivalent to a gross return of 9.56% in a 50% tax bracket.

The following table illustrates what investors in various tax brackets would have to earn to net 4.78%.

Your Top Income Tax Bracket Filing Jointly	Gross Interest Return to Net 4.78%
32%	7.03%
36%	7.47%
39%	7.84%
42%	8.24%
48%	9.19%
50%	9.56%
60%	11.95%
70%	15.93%

As you can see, the higher your income tax bracket, the more attractive insurance becomes as an investment.

Benjamin Graham, co-author of one of the investment

industry's most respected texts, commented that Mr. Linton's study illustrates the value of cash value life insurance as an alternative to the bond component of an individual's investment portfolio.* This is quite a tribute to life insurance as an investment; however, it only becomes an investment after it is seasoned. An insurance policy is primarily a protective device. The investment aspects need only be considered when determining what type of insurance to acquire.

Minimum Deposit—Another popular concept today is minimum deposit life insurance. Under this approach, you borrow the cash values from your permanent policy each year to pay the premium on that policy. In order to deduct interest on the policy loans, the insured must pay four of the first seven annual premiums out of his own pocket. Once he has paid the four premiums, his primary cost for the insurance is the deductible interest on the loan. Some companies have designed high early cash value contracts to accommodate this concept, but most companies attempt to restrict the proliferation of minimum deposit insurance because it reduces their investment assets and, consequently, reduces their earnings. The biggest criticism I have of the minimum deposit concept is that it cannot be continued indefinitely. At some point the interest on the loan will exceed the cost of protection. The insurance will probably be dropped when this occurs and the proceeds unavailable when needed most. The only way the insurance can be kept in force indefinitely is if the loan is repaid at some point.

Accidental Death Coverage—This insurance provides benefits only if you die as a result of an accident. Inasmuch as accidental death is relatively rare in all age brackets, the premiums are quite low. Before you invest in accidental death protection, make certain you have acquired all the

**U.S. News & World Report,* October 7, 1963, page 102.

insurance you need to protect your family in the event of death from all causes.

Credit Life Insurance—Credit life insurance is usually sold by banks, finance companies, and others who lend money. It is designed to pay the lender off in the event you pass away before the loan is paid. This is fairly expensive term insurance. For example, a man age forty can obtain one year renewable term insurance from a regular life insurance company for about $3 per thousand. A typical credit life policy might cost him about $12 per thousand. You would be better off acquiring additional insurance from your personal life insurance advisor and assigning it to your creditors than buying credit life.

Disability Waiver of Premiums—This is an important rider to have attached to any insurance policy. It provides that if you become totally disabled, your premiums will be paid automatically as long as that disability continues. Of course, your cash values continue to grow and are available to you whenever you need them.

CONCLUSION

There are many other facets of life insurance beyond the scope of this book. It is a complicated subject. A buyer should either attempt to learn all he can about life insurance in general or select an agent who is knowledgeable and in whom he has confidence to select the proper insurance for him. In this regard, CLU's (chartered life underwriters) are among the more knowledgeable agents. They are required to pass a comprehensive study course in order to obtain the CLU designation.

CHAPTER XIII

SETTLEMENT OPTIONS

Settlement options are a systematic method of liquidating principal in equal installments over a number of years or a lifetime. The concept of settlement options arose because proceeds payable in a lump sum were often dissipated over a relatively short period of time. There was an obvious need for safety of principal and amounts of income beyond what could be provided by interest alone.

ADVANTAGES

There are several advantages incident to the use of settlement options. First, they provide certain unconditional guarantees. Beneficiaries know they will always receive at least the amount of interest and principal specified in the contract. In addition, excess interest is usually paid over and above the guaranteed rate.

The second advantage is one of simplicity. A fixed amount of income is paid to the beneficiary each month and he has no responsibility for investment supervision.

Finally, the proceeds of the insurance are protected. Creditors of the beneficiaries and, under certain circumstances, of the insured are precluded from reaching them. The beneficiaries cannot make speculative investments with the proceeds or simply spend at an imprudent rate.

DISADVANTAGES

There are also a few possible disadvantages of settlement options. Safety of principal cannot be obtained merely by holding a specific dollar amount. The purchasing power of that principal also needs to be taken into account. A fixed return of $200 per month in 1940 would have provided a comfortable living for a widow, but that same $200 per month today might not pay her rent.

The other obvious disadvantage is that beneficiaries under fifty years of age will normally realize as much income from interest on a savings account as they will under an income option.

TRENDS IN SETTLEMENT OPTION PLANNING

There is far less planning with options today than twenty years ago. The trend has been toward simplicity and flexibility. Most agents suggest their clients leave the proceeds under the interest option which allows the beneficiaries to either select one of the other options or withdraw the proceeds.

ALTERNATIVE SETTLEMENT OPTIONS AVAILABLE

Lump Sum Distribution—A lump sum distribution is self-explanatory. This is the normal situation in which the proceeds are paid to the beneficiary in one lump sum. It is a simple method of distribution which gives the beneficiary complete flexibility. There are a few possible disadvantages we should review. First, there is no protection from the beneficiary's creditors. Second, some companies will not pay interest from the date of death to the date of payment. If payment is not claimed quickly or legal entanglements make the proceeds difficult to collect, a considerable amount of interest might be lost. Finally, if the insured and the beneficiary are killed in a common disaster, or the beneficiary dies shortly thereafter, the proceeds might end up in the beneficiary's estate. Most good insurance men protect against this problem by naming a contingent beneficiary and including a common disaster clause in the contract.

Interest Option—This option provides that the proceeds will be held by the company and interest paid to the beneficiary. The beneficiary can be given the right to withdraw all or part of the proceeds, name beneficiaries of the residue, or select another option. To the extent the beneficiary cannot withdraw proceeds, it is usually protected from his creditors. There are two possible disadvantages to the interest option. First, principal can only be kept intact for a specified number of years. The specific period varies with state laws and company practices. Second, interest must be paid out at least annually. It cannot be accumulated. In many instances, it is desirable not to make distributions in particular years. About the only way you can withhold them is to create a trust.

Fixed Period Option—The fixed period provides that a certain amount will be paid each month over a set period of time. For example, $100 per month for 120 months. This option is normally used to fill a short term need. This option results in a loss of flexibility. Most companies will not allow principal withdrawals, and if they are allowed future payments are reduced. For example, a principal sum of $10,000 might generate $100 per month for ten years. If at the end of two years $2,000 is withdrawn to meet an emergency, payments for the remaining eight years might be reduced to $70 per month.

Fixed Amount Option—This option provides for a fixed amount for as long as the proceeds last. This is slightly more flexible than the fixed period option in that the monthly income can be varied in anticipation of beneficiaries' changing needs. A widow, for example, will receive social security while the children are growing up, but once they are out on their own she receives nothing until she is at least sixty-two years of age. The options could be designed to pay her $X per month while she is receiving social security payments and $2X when the social security runs out. Beneficiaries can have the right to withdraw principal, but each withdrawal will result in shortening the payment period. Using the example we used to describe the fixed period option, the difference becomes evident. We start off with a principal sum of $10,000 payable over ten years at a rate of $100 per month. If, under the fixed amount option, a withdrawal of $2,000 is made at the end of two years, the $100 per month will continue, but the period will be shortened to eight years.

Life Income Option—The beneficiary's life expectancy is determined and an amount actuarially calculated that will enable the proceeds to be paid out in equal installments over the beneficiary's lifetime. There are four variations to the life income option.

1. **No Refund Option**—This option provides the greatest income return to the beneficiary, but if he does not reach his life expectancy, any remaining principal reverts to the insurance company.
2. **Refund Option**—If the face amount of the contract has not been paid to the beneficiary, when that beneficiary dies the remaining principal is paid to a contingent beneficiary. For example, a $10,000 policy is payable at a rate of $120 per month to a beneficiary with a nine-year life expectancy. The beneficiary dies after receiving payments for twenty months. The contingent beneficiary receives $7,600 under the refund option.

Face amount	$10,000
$120 × 20 months	2,400
Refund	$7,600

3. Period Certain Option—Under this option, a certain number of installments are guaranteed, usually 120 months or 240 months. If the primary beneficiary dies before receiving the guaranteed number of payments, payments are continued for a contingent beneficiary until the end of the guarantee period. A $10,000 policy is payable $120 per month for life with a 120-month guarantee. The beneficiary dies at the end of twenty months. The contingent beneficiary will receive $12,000 (100 months × $120).

4. Joint and Survivor Option—This option provides for the annuity payments to continue for more than one lifetime. Payments are somewhat lower than they would be on a single life.

The advantage of life income options is that the payments are guaranteed for the beneficiary's lifetime. There is no way the benefits can be outlived. The disadvantages are a lack of flexibility, and loss of purchasing power if inflation continues.

Excess Interest—Many companies provide for increased or extended benefits by crediting option plans and annuities with part of the excess interest earned above what is assumed in calculating the benefits.

CONCLUSION

Settlement options provide certain guarantees which cannot be obtained with any other plan of distribution; however, those guarantees result in a loss of flexibility. In situations where you are interested in providing fixed amounts for specific periods of time, settlement options may be your best solution.

CHAPTER XIV

TAXATION OF LIFE INSURANCE

Many people are operating under the fallacious assumption that life insurance is not taxable. Nothing could be further from the truth. Under certain circumstances the proceeds will be subjected to either income taxation or estate taxation, and under other circumstances they will be free from taxation of either type. The purpose of this chapter is to illustrate the various tax consequences of all aspects of life insurance.

TAX DEDUCTIBILITY OF LIFE INSURANCE PREMIUMS

The general rule is that life insurance premiums are non-deductible either by an individual or a corporation; however, there are certain exceptions to this rule. Premiums paid by an employer as part of a plan of group life insurance are deductible by the employer. Such employer-paid group insurance premiums are income tax free to the employee except to the extent the insurance exceeds $50,000 of face value. To the extent the face amount exceeds $50,000, the employee will be treated as having received reportable income based on the following table reduced by the employee's contribution:

Age	Cost per $1,000 of Coverage per Month	Annual Cost per $1,000
Under 30	$ .08	$ .96
30–34	.10	1.20
35–39	.14	1.68
40–44	.23	2.76
45–49	.40	4.80
50–54	.68	8.16
55–59	1.10	13.20
60–64	1.63	19.56

Example: Assume an employee age forty-seven is entitled to $100,000 of coverage under his company's group plan. He contributes $2 per thousand per year and the company pays the balance. That employee's taxable income would be calculated as follows:

Total group insurance	$100,000	
Less tax free portion	50,000	
Excess coverage	$ 50,000	
Annual cost from table	×4.80	per thousand
Total annual cost of excess	240.00	
Employee's contribution ($100,000 × $2 per thousand)	200.00	
Amount taxable to employee	$ 40.00	

TAXATION OF DIVIDENDS

Dividends are normally tax exempt because they represent a return of capital. If dividends are left to accumulate in the policy, the interest on those accumulated dividends is taxable in the year in which it is earned.

DEDUCTIBILITY OF INTEREST ON POLICY LOANS

Interest on policy loans is usually deductible, but it must actually be paid. It cannot be deducted if it is allowed to increase the loan. Also, interest cannot be deducted if it is part of a plan to purchase which consists of systematic borrowings (minimum deposit); however, there are several exceptions to this general rule on systematic borrowing:

1. Interest is deductible if the owner pays four of the first seven annual premiums without borrowing.
2. It is deductible if it does not exceed $100.
3. It is deductible if the loan was made because of the taxpayer's unforeseen loss of income or an increase in his financial obligations.
4. Interest is deductible if the loan is in connection with the taxpayer's trade or business.

TAXATION OF PROCEEDS

Income Taxation—There will be no income tax payable by a beneficiary upon receipt of insurance proceeds unless the policy was transferred to the beneficiary for valuable consideration. An example of this would be where Mr. A sells an existing $10,000 policy on his life to Mr. B for $4,000. Mr. B pays an additional $500 of premiums prior to Mr. A's death. Upon Mr. A's death the difference between the proceeds ($10,000) and Mr. B's investment in the contract ($4,000 initial investment and $500 of subsequent premiums) would be taxable to Mr. B. The taxable amount would be $10,000 − $4,500, or $5,500. There are several exceptions to the transfer for value rule. A transfer to the insured, a partner of the insured, a partnership in which the insured is a partner, or a corporation in which the insured is a shareholder or officer would be exempt from the transfer for value rule. There is also an exception which relates to tax-free incorporation or reorganizations, but that is beyond the scope of this text.

DEATH TAXATION

The Federal Estate Tax—Generally speaking, the proceeds of life insurance are taxable in the insured's estate if he holds any incidents of ownership in the policy or the proceeds are payable to or for the benefit of his estate. Obviously, if the insured is the absolute owner of the policy it will be included in his estate. If someone else is the named owner but the insured or his estate have a right to the economic benefits of the policy, it will be included. If the insured has the right to control the beneficial enjoyment of the policy (change beneficiaries or modes of settlement) it will be included. If the decedent owns policies on the lives of other people, the fair market value of those policies will be included in his estate. Fair market value will normally approximate cash value.

In community property states, the policy is presumed to be community property unless the spouses have intentionally provided otherwise; consequently only one-half of the proceeds would be included in the insured spouse's estate. If the non-insured spouse dies first, one-half the fair market value would be included.

The proceeds of any policy owned by a corporation will tend to increase the value of a sole or controlling shareholder's stock. For example, if Mr. X, who owned 65% of the XYZ company which has a fair market value of $1,000,000, dies, and the company receives $100,000 of insurance proceeds, the IRS will attempt to increase the value of his stock by $65,000. His interest in the business would be valued at $715,000 instead of $650,000.

Proceeds payable to a surviving spouse qualify for the estate tax marital deduction if that spouse has the right to take them in a lump sum or if payments under a settlement option are to the spouse or the spouse's estate. A contingent beneficiary can be named and the proceeds will still qualify for the marital deduction as long as the surviving spouse has a general power of appointment.

State Death Taxes—Many states allow a certain amount of insurance to pass to named beneficiaries tax free. Check with your local advisors to determine taxation of proceeds in your state.

TAX ASPECTS OF SETTLEMENT OPTIONS

The options discussed in the prior chapter are available either to the insured during his lifetime or to his beneficiaries after his death.

Proceeds Payable During Lifetime—There are two situations in which an insured can elect to use the cash in his insurance policies to provide him with income: when an endowment contract matures or when he decides to use the accumulated cash values in his ordinary life contract. If he withdraws the cash in a lump sum, any gain over his investment in the contract will be taxable to him as ordinary income. In calculating his investment, dividends paid to him and the portion of premiums paid for disability waiver of premium and accidental death benefits are deducted from the total premiums paid.

Example: Ten-year endowment

Cash value at maturity			$10,000
Investment:			
Ten years' premiums at $1,000 per year		$10,000	
Less:			
Dividends received	$1,000		
Disability waiver	500		
Accidental death	500		
		2,000	
Net investment in contract			8,000
Taxable as ordinary income			$2,000

If an installment option is elected within sixty days of maturity, the tax can be deferred over the life of the option. An exclusion ratio (amount free of tax) will be determined by dividing the investment in the contract by the number of years over which payments can be anticipated.

> **Example:** Assume a ten-year fixed income option is elected which provides for payments of $120 per month.

Exclusion ratio = $8,000 ÷ 10 = $800 per year	
Annual income ($120 × 12)	$1440
Exclusion	800
Taxable income	$640

Proceeds Payable Upon Death. Interest Only Option—If the policy is held by the company under the interest option, only the interest is taxable to the beneficiary.

Installment Options—The total proceeds are divided by the number of installments anticipated in order to determine the excludible portion of each payment. The balance of each payment is taxable as ordinary income.

> **Example:** Assume a widow age seventy has a life expectancy of fifteen years. Her husband dies and leaves her a $24,000 life insurance policy on which she elects to receive payments of $2,000 per year for life.

Annual income	$2000
Exclusion ratio = $24,000 ÷ 15 =	$1600 per year
Taxable income	$ 400

Interest Exclusion—An extremely beneficial feature of settlement options is the surviving spouse's right to exclude the first $1,000 of interest received each year. This applies only to those options which use both income and principal to make the payments. If the policy in the preceding example were the only policy on settlement options, there would be no taxable income.

CONCLUSION

Life insurance is taxable under certain circumstances both for income tax and estate tax purposes. The lesson to be learned from this chapter is that no policy should be acquired or changed until you have ascertained what the tax consequences might be.

CHAPTER XV

CHARITABLE GIFTS

Charitable gifts are not just for the wealthy. Many people of modest means can benefit significantly by transferring assets to their favorite charities. People make gifts to charity for many reasons. Some are primarily concerned with supporting a particular charitable organization while others make gifts to obtain income or estate tax savings.

In most instances the desire to benefit a particular charity exists before the other reasons become important; however, we will provide examples of situations where transfers to charity can satisfy purely selfish objectives.

LIFETIME GIFTS TO CHARITY

Outright Gift—Individuals in high income tax brackets can obtain certain advantages through the transfer of assets direct to a charity.

Example: Dorothy Donor in a 60% tax bracket owns stock valued at $10,000 for which she paid $2,000. If she were to sell that stock she would realize an $8,000 capital gain and be subjected to state and federal taxes of approximately $2,500. Dorothy would net $7,500 after taxes. If Dorothy contributes the stock to her favorite charity, she becomes entitled to a $10,000 income tax deduction. Since she is in a 60% tax bracket, the gift will save her $6,000 in taxes. Dorothy's gift of $10,000 worth of stock was made at a cost to her of $1,500, the difference between the $7,500 after tax proceeds of sale and the $6,000 tax savings resulting from the gift.

Remainder Interest Gifts—A remainder interest gift is one in which you donate an asset to a charity, but retain the right to an income for the rest of your life or a specified period of time. Individuals do not have to be in extremely high income tax brackets to benefit from this type of gift. By transferring a remainder interest you obtain an immediate income tax deduction, and at the same time retain the income from the property for the rest of your life. Basically, there are three types of charitable remainder gifts: the charitable remainder annuity trust, the charitable remainder unitrust, and the pooled income fund.

The Annuity Trust is one in which a fixed amount (at least 5% of the initial principal) is paid at least annually to one or more people for a term of years (not more than twenty) or for the lifetimes of such persons.

Example: Phil N. Thropic is fifty years old. His taxable income is $40,000 and his top tax bracket is 48%. Phil decides to place $50,000 of assets in an annuity trust which will pay him 6% or $3,000 each year. The value of the charitable remainder interest is .35970. This results in an income tax deduction of approximately $18,000 (.36 × $50,000) and tax savings in the present year of $8,640 ($18,000 × 48). In addition, any capital gains resulting from the sale of assets transferred to the trust will be taxable to the charity and not to Mr. Thropic.

The Unitrust is similar to the annuity trust except that the amount distributed annually will fluctuate with the value of the trust each year. The trust can provide that if the income is less than the required percentage, only the income itself must be paid out. This avoids the necessity to invade principal in a given year. If income in a subsequent year exceeds the stated percentage, the trust can provide that any deficit be made up.

Example: Assume Phil creates a unitrust instead of an annuity trust. He would obtain the same income tax benefits, but instead of receiving a fixed amount of $3,000 per year, he would receive varying amounts. The following table illustrates what might occur:

Year	Principal	Income Earned	6%	Amount Paid	Deficit
1	$50,000	$3,000	$3,000	$3,000	–0–
2	55,000	3,000	3,300	3,000	$300
3	60,000	3,500	3,600	3,500	400
4	55,000	3,500	3,300	3,500	200
5	60,000	4,000	3,600	3,800	–0–
6	65,000	4,000	3,900	3,900	–0–
7	70,000	4,000	4,200	4,000	200
8	65,000	4,000	3,900	4,000	100
9	70,000	4,200	4,200	4,200	100
10	80,000	5,000	4,800	4,900	–0–

Neither the annuity trust nor the unitrust can provide for emergency invasions of principal or all benefits will be lost. These trusts can extend for more than one lifetime. A husband and wife, for example, could reserve the right to the income for their joint lifetimes. The value of the remainder interest and, consequently, the amount of deduction would be reduced somewhat due to the probability of one of the individuals exceeding his life expectancy.

Pooled Income Funds are normally created by the charities themselves. A donor's funds are commingled with those of other donors and distributions made from the fund in a manner similar to distributions from unitrusts and annuity trusts.

Some individuals prefer having the ability to tailor trusts to satisfy specific goals such as endowing a chair at a university or providing funds for research in a particular area. Others are content with letting the charity handle funds as it sees fit. In the latter situation a pooled income fund may suffice.

CONVERTING TAXABLE INCOME TO TAX-FREE INCOME

Some tax practitioners suggest that securities producing taxable interest or dividends be transferred into charitable remainder trusts. Once those securities are in the trust, the trustee can sell them and reinvest the proceeds in tax-exempt bonds. This conversion of taxable income to non-taxable income significantly increases the benefits to the donor.

Pooled income funds are restricted from investing in tax-exempt securities, while there is no express prohibition relating to unitrusts and annuity trusts. The trustee cannot, however, be required to convert to tax-exempt bonds or the gain from the sale of the original assets will be taxable to the donor.

TAXATION OF DISTRIBUTION

Income from the annuity or unitrust is considered to be distributed in a specified manner. Distributions are first treated as ordinary income to the extent of the trust's ordinary income for the year and undistributed ordinary income for prior years. Second, long-term capital gains realized by the trust are considered as having been distributed. Next, tax-exempt income is presumed to be distributed and finally, if additional distributions are needed they will be treated as tax-free returns of principal.

Example: Mr. Al Truist funds a charitable remainder annuity trust with $50,000 of common stocks generating $1,500 a year and $50,000 of municipal bonds generating $2,500 per year. During the first year $10,000 of common stocks having a basis of $7,000 are sold by the trustee. The trust provides for $5,000 to be distributed to Mr. Truist. The tax status of his income would be determined as follows:

Ordinary income	$1,500
Capital gains	3,000
Tax-free income	500
Total distribution	$5,000

TESTAMENTARY GIFTS TO CHARITY

Testamentary gifts can also be made outright or in trust. They can provide a means of minimizing estate taxes and are particularly valuable to childless married couples.

Example: Mr. and Mrs. E. Lee Mosynary have a $600,000 estate. They have no children and no close relatives. Mr. Mosynary plans to leave everything to his wife if she survives him and then to some distant relatives on both sides. He is not particularly concerned about those relatives but doesn't know who else to leave it to. His attorney advises him the estate will be subject to $40,800 of taxes on his death and $131,000 on Mrs. Mosynary's death. Mr. Mosynary is appalled. He feels he has paid handsome income taxes all his life and does not want the government to receive any more than necessary after his death. The attorney suggests that Lee put one-half of the estate in a charitable remainder unitrust with Mrs. Mosynary, who is sixty-nine years old, receiving the income. Under this plan there would be no taxes on the first death which would result in Mrs. Mosynary receiving approximately $2,500 per year of additional income because the tax on Mr. Mosynary's death would be eliminated by the charitable deductions. The taxes on the second death would be reduced to $40,800.

HYBRID-GIFTS OF LIFE INSURANCE

Many people like to make gifts of life insurance because a relatively low premium can result in a fairly substantial gift. If the charity is named owner of the policy or irrevocable beneficiary, the insured is entitled to a current income tax deduction. Where the charity is named owner of a permanent policy, the cash values are available for current use by the charity if it needs them. For example, assume the annual premium on a $10,000 policy is $200. The average annual increase in cash value might be $150. The charity could withdraw the $150 each year for current expenses.

Properly set up, gifts of life insurance may provide a double deduction. By naming the charity as irrevocable beneficiary instead of owner and restricting the insured-owner's rights, the premiums may be deductible for income tax purposes and the proceeds deductible for estate tax purposes. The estate tax charitable deduction will also increase the marital deduction in husband-wife situations.

Example: Dr. Don A. Shun has an estate of $700,000. He wants Mrs. Shun to have the use of as much of the estate as possible when he passes away. His attorney tells him there will be $57,800 of estate taxes on his death. This upsets Don and he mentions the problem to his insurance man who suggests Don purchase a life insurance policy in which his medical school is named irrevocable beneficiary. The charitable gift will increase the marital deduction and reduce estate taxes. They calculate he will need $350,000 of insurance to eliminate the entire estate tax.

	Before Insurance	*After Insurance*
Adj. gross estate	$700,000	$1,050,000
Marital deduction	350,000	525,000
	350,000	525,000
Charitable deduction	-0-	350,000
Taxable	350,000	175,000
Estate tax	$104,800	$46,800
Less unified credit	47,000	47,000
Tax payable	$57,800	$-0-

This idea appeals to Don. He has been giving his school $2,500 a year anyway and the insurance will give him a double deduction. The agent suggests a combination of permanent and term insurance which will cost Don $5,000 a year. His additional after-tax cost from implementing this plan would be $1,250 per year. Don considers this to be a fairly reasonable cost to eliminate the estate taxes, and he would prefer for his university to have the money than to have it go to the government.

The following table illustrates the face amount of insurance necessary in various size estates to eliminate the federal estate tax on the first death. The table ignores other estate settlement costs and state death taxes.

If the donor is not interested in making current deductible gifts to charity, he can merely name the charity as beneficiary of the policy. Under this approach he will have complete access to the cash values and can use them in whatever way he desires without losing the estate tax deduction.

Charitable Insurance Required to Avoid Estate Tax

	Before Insurance		After Insurance			
Gross Estate	Amount of Tax	Insurance Amount	New Gross Estate	Marital Deduction	Taxable Estate	Tax
400,000	7,800	50,000	450,000	225,000	175,000	–0–
500,000	23,800	150,000	750,000	325,000	175,000	–0–
600,000	40,800	250,000	850,000	425,000	175,000	–0–
700,000	57,800	350,000	1,050,000	525,000	175,000	–0–
800,000	74,800	450,000	1,250,000	625,000	175,000	–0–
900,000	91,800	550,000	1,450,000	725,000	175,000	–0–
1,000,000	108,800	650,000	1,650,000	825,000	175,000	–0–

LIMITATIONS ON INCOME TAX DEDUCTIONS

The amount of annual deduction you can take depends upon the type of property you are contributing, the type of organization to which it is being contributed, and the use that organization will be making of it. For purposes of this discussion we will assume all gifts are made to qualifying public charities.

Contributions of cash and property in which there are no capital gains qualify for a deduction up to 50% of your adjusted gross income computed without regard to any operating loss carryback. In most instances, adjusted gross income will be the basis for any deduction.

Appreciated securities, other intangible personal property, and real estate held long-term are limited to a 30% deduction. The 30% ceiling also applies to appreciated tangible personal property like art, antiques, automobiles, etc., when the charity's use of the property is directly related to its charitable purpose. For example, a gift of art to a museum would qualify.

If tangible personal property is given to an organization whose use of the gift is not related to charitable purposes, a different set of limits applies. Gifts of this type will qualify for the 50% ceiling; however, the amount of deduction will be reduced by 50% of the appreciation.

> **Example:** Mr. Art Critic owns a painting valued at \$15,000 for which he paid \$6,000 ten years ago. His adjusted gross income is \$25,000. If he gives the painting to the Art Institute, his deduction is limited to 30% or \$7,500. If he gives it to the United Fund, he qualifies for the 50% ceiling and can deduct the market value less 50% of the appreciation or \$10,500 ($\$15{,}000 - \frac{(15{,}000 - 6{,}000)}{2} = \$10{,}500$).

Contributors of intangible personal property can elect to reduce their deduction by 50% of the appreciation and also qualify for the 50% ceiling. Each individual should consult with his tax advisor to determine the effects of any particular type of gift. There are no limitations related to testamentary charitable gifts. One hundred percent of your estate can be given to charity free of estate tax.

CONCLUSION

Charitable gifts, properly utilized, can increase a family's spendable income; however, in most instances, the desire to provide for a particular charity must exist before a gift makes sense. Remainder interest gifts can provide current income tax benefits without seriously impairing enjoyment of the asset given to the charity, and gifts of life insurance can reduce taxes through increasing the marital deduction.

CHAPTER XVI

FAMILY PARTNERSHIPS AND CORPORATIONS

High income individuals are always looking for ways to minimize income taxes. Family partnerships and corporations provide the high bracket owner with viable approaches to saving income taxes. They can also facilitate distribution of the estate and reduce estate taxes.

THE FAMILY PARTNERSHIP

Family partnerships provide a unique opportunity for several family members to enjoy the income from the family business. As with all estate planning tools, there are advantages and disadvantages.

Advantages of Family Partnerships

1. Interests in the family business can be transferred to both adult and minor beneficiaries with relative ease.
2. The value of these transfers up to $3,000 per donee per year will be free of federal gift and estate tax.
3. Each partner's share of the income will be taxable to that partner, thereby creating additional income tax pockets.

4. The transferring partner can continue to manage the business.

Example—Mrs. Ruby Diamond owns a flourishing jewelry store on Park Avenue. She is currently earning $100,000 per year and would like to transfer some of that income to her four children, their spouses, and her eight grandchildren. Her CPA advises her that a business such as hers would sell for about $250,000, plus the inventory. The net value of inventory is another $250,000; consequently the total value of the business is $500,000. The CPA and attorney got their heads together and decided Ruby should create a limited partnership. She would be the general partner during her lifetime and manage the business as she has always done. Her children, in-laws, and grandchildren would become limited partners. Ruby will receive a management salary of $30,000 and each of the partners will share in the income in proportion to their ownership interest. In the first year Ruby transferred approximately 9.6% of the business to her family ($3,000 gift to each of sixteen individuals or a total of $48,000). This reduced her taxable income in that year to $93,280, calculated as follows:

Total earnings	$100,000	
Salary	30,000	$ 30,000
Divisible by partners	70,000	
Limited partner's share @ 9.6%	6,720	
Ruby's share	$ 63,280	63,280
Ruby's taxable income		$ 93,280

The first year's savings is not too significant; however, if Ruby transfers 9.6% each year for eight years, only

23.2% will be included in her estate and as general partner she will continue to manage the business. Her taxable income would be reduced to:

Total earnings	$100,000	
Salary	30,000	$30,000
Divisible by partners	70,000	
Limited partner's share @ 76.8%	53,760	
Ruby's share	16,240	16,240
Ruby's taxable income		$46,240

Each of the limited partners would receive $3,360 which will be taxed in their relatively low tax brackets. Equally as important, Ruby will have transferred $384,000 out of her taxable estate ($500,000 × .768) without giving up control of the business. If the jewelry store continues to grow, the amount effectively transferred may be considerably greater.

DISADVANTAGES OF FAMILY PARTNERSHIPS

1. If the business is operated as a general partnership, the assets of all family members will be subject to attack by creditors.
2. The income tax rules governing family partnerships are stringent and must be closely adhered to by the doner-partner.

   a. The creation of the family partnership and its continuing operation must be motivated by business considerations and not simply as a tax avoidance device.
   b. If the donor-partner exercises unreasonable control, all of the income will be taxable to him.

c. Capital must be a material income producing factor. An interest in a personal service business such as medicine, law, or insurance would probably not qualify.
d. The donor must be reasonably compensated for his activities as manager.
e. A minor's interest must be held for him by an independent trustee or guardian.
f. The IRS could create havoc by attributing a higher value to the gifts than was originally anticipated.

THE FAMILY CORPORATION

The primary difference between corporations and partnerships is the extent of personal liability incurred by the owners and the way in which they are taxed. The liability of corporate shareholders is usually limited to their investment in the corporation. This is also true of limited partners; however, general partners are personally liable for all debts of the partnership.

A corporation is a separate tax paying entity while a partnership is not. If A and B go into business as partners, all the income of that partnership will be reported on A and B's income tax returns. On the other hand, if they form the AB Corporation, A and B would be taxed on the salaries they receive and the balance of the income would be taxed to the AB Corporation. Any other distributions from the corporation would be treated as dividends and subject to double taxation since they represent earnings previously taxed to the corporation.

Corporate tax rates may be lower than the tax rates to which the owners are subject. Assume A and B generate income from the business of $120,000. If $50,000 is distributed to each, they will be in 50% tax brackets and any additional amounts they receive will be taxed at 50¢ on the dollar. If the remaining $20,000 is left in the corporation, they may only pay tax at the rate of 22%. Since most businessmen invest part of their income back into the business, they might as well take advantage of the lower corporate tax rates. Incidentally, salaries to corporate stockholders must be reasonable and compensate for the actual work performed or the excess amount, over what is reasonable, will be treated as dividends and taxed to the corporation.

There is a subsection of the tax law referred to as Subchapter S which allows corporations meeting certain conditions to have their earnings taxed directly to the stockholders. The result is a form of ownership similar to a partnership with the advantages of a limited liability.

CORPORATIONS ALLOW DIFFERENT BENEFITS FOR FAMILY MEMBERS WITH DIFFERING NEEDS:

Active Employees—Those family members who are active in the business can qualify for group insurance, substantial retirement benefits, medical reimbursement plans, and many other tax deductible fringe benefits.

Non-Active Stockholders—It is possible through the corporate structure to provide certain family members with income and allow others to participate in the growth. The corporation could create two classes of stock: dividend-paying preferred stock and non-dividend-paying common stock. Older family members who need income can be given the preferred. Younger family members and those managing the business could be given the common stock.

CONCLUSION

The decision as to whether a family should consider a partnership or corporation is complex and requires a knowledgeable attorney and CPA to analyze all of the ramifications. Each situation is unique and what is desirable for one family may not be desirable for others.

CHAPTER XVII

THE PRIVATE ANNUITY

The private annuity is a rarely used device which, under certain circumstances, can remove assets from the estate owner's gross estate free of gift or estate taxation. By definition, a private annuity is an unsecured promise made by an individual, corporation, or charitable organization (the payor) to make fixed payments to another individual (the annuitant) for his lifetime in return for the transfer of certain assets (real estate, securities, cash, and so forth) from the annuitant to the payor.

A typical plan might contemplate that a father will transfer appreciated rental property to his son in exchange for the son's promise to pay father a fixed amount each month for the rest of father's life. The transaction is treated as a sale in which the consideration is not cash or a note but rather the son's promise to pay his father an annuity for life.

The private annuity has the following advantages:

1. Assets are removed from the annuitant's estate and replaced by an annuity which will have no value once the annuitant passes away. As a result, neither the asset itself nor the annuity will be included in the annuitant's taxable estate.
2. No part of the transaction will be treated as a gift if

the present value of the anticipated annuity payments equals the value of the property.

3. The sale of appreciated property results in some capital gain. Under the private annuity, capital gain taxes are deferred and payable over the annuitant's lifetime.
4. The annuitant will have a fixed income for life.

The results of a private annuity are not always positive. There are these possible disadvantages:

1. The primary disadvantage of the private annuity to the annuitant is that he has no guarantee the payor will be able to continue the payments. The annuitant is not allowed to retain any type of security interest (trust deed, etc.) in the property or the property will be included in his estate.
2. A disadvantage to the payor is that the annuitant might outlive his life expectancy which would result in the payor paying more for the property than it is actually worth.
3. The values of both the property and the annuity are subject to question. While listed securities are easy to value, real estate and closely held stock pose problems. A qualified appraiser should be retained to evaluate this type of asset. The amount of the annuity payment consistent with the value of the property can be obtained by checking the government's tables under Reg. 20.2031.7. For example, if the property is valued at $100,000 and the annuitant is age seventy, the amount of the annual annuity would be obtained by dividing $100,000 by 6.8823 which would result in a payment of $14,530 year year. If the payment is less than this amount, the annuitant will be treated as having made a gift to the payor. If instead of $14,500, for example, the annuitant only takes an income of $12,000, the annuity would be valued at $82,587

(12,000 × 6.8823). The difference of $17,413 would be treated as a gift from the annuitant to the payor.

4. The payor will be taxed on any income generated by the property; however, he will not be allowed to deduct any part of the annuity payments because they are considered to be part of the purchase price of the property.
5. The annuitant is usually of an age where the annuity payments will exceed the income generated by the property resulting in a cash flow problem for the payor. For example, the property may be generating $1,000 per month of income, but if the annuity payment is $1,200, the extra $200 will have to come out of the payor's pocket.
6. If the annuitant dies within a few years, the payor will have a very low cost basis.

TAX CONSEQUENCES TO THE ANNUITANT

Death Tax Consequences—The transferred property is excluded from the annuitant's estate for purposes of the unified transfer tax. Since the annuity terminates at death, it also avoids taxation.

Income Tax Consequences—There are three elements in each payment received by the annuitant: the recovery of basis element, the gain element, and the annuity element.

The Recovery of Basis Element (Exclusion Ratio)—This portion of each payment is tax free to the annuitant and is calculated as follows:

$$\text{Exclusion ratio} = \frac{\text{Cost basis of property}}{\text{Total expected return}}$$

The cost basis is the annuitant's cost adjusted for depreciation, improvements, and so forth. The total expected return is one year's annuity payment multiplied by the annuitant's life expectancy.

As an example, assume Cash Greenback, age seventy, transfers rental property having a fair market value of $100,000 and a cost basis of $40,000 to his son, Buck, in exchange for a private annuity. The annuity factor for a man age seventy, as you will recall, is 6.8823. To calculate the annual annuity payment, you divide the market value of the property by the annuity factor: $100,000 ÷ 6.8823 = $14,530. Buck would have to pay his father $14,530 per year for his father's lifetime in order for the annuity to be equivalent to the value of the property. Once the amount of the annuity payment has been ascertained, the next step is to determine the portion of the annuity payment which represents a recovery of Cash's basis and is tax free. Cash has a life expectancy of 12.1 years. The "total expected return" from the annuity is calculated by multiplying the annual payment by his life expectancy (12.1 × 14,530). The total expected return would be $175,813. Going back to our formula for calculating the Exclusion ratio:

$$\text{Exclusion ratio} = \frac{\text{Cost basis of property}}{\text{Total expected return}} = \frac{\$40{,}000}{\$175{,}813} = .2275\%$$

The excludible amount of each payment is determined by multiplying the annual payment by the exclusion ratio: $14,530 × .2275 = $3,305.57 which represents the tax-free portion of each payment.

Gain Element—The gain element represents the excess of fair market value over cost. This gain is reported ratably over the annuitant's life expectancy and treated as capital gain for tax purposes. If the annuitant survives his life expectancy, the gain portion of subsequent payments will be treated as ordinary income.

Example: The gain element is calculated by dividing the gain over cost by the annuitant's life expectancy:

$$\text{Gain element} = \frac{\$100{,}000 - \$40{,}000}{12.1} = \frac{\$60{,}000}{12.1} = \$4{,}958.68$$

For the first twelve years, $4,958.68 of each payment will be treated as capital gain. In the thirteenth year, $495.87 will be considered capital gain.

Annuity Element—The balance of each annuity payment, known as the annuity element, will be taxed as ordinary income. For the first twelve years, the payments will be taxed as follows:

Recovery of basis	$ 3,305.57
Capital gain	4,958.68
Ordinary income	6,265.75
Total payment	$14,530.00

In the thirteenth year, the payments will be treated as:

Recovery of basis	$ 3,305.57
Capital gain	495.87
Ordinary income	10,728.56
Total payment	$14,530.00

In the fourteenth year and each year thereafter, the payments will be taxed as follows:

Recovery of basis	$ 3,305.57
Ordinary income	11,224.43
Total payment	$14,530.00

TAX CONSEQUENCES TO THE PAYOR

As was mentioned earlier, the payor will be receiving taxable income from the property, but he cannot deduct the payments to the annuitant. Depending upon his personal financial situation and the nature of the property transferred, this could be disastrous.

If the annuitant dies early, the payor's cost basis will be quite low. In the previous example, if the annuitant, Cash Greenback, had died at the end of the third year, Buck would have a cost basis in the property of $43,590 (14,530 × 3).

There are some potentially serious problems related to the payor's estate. If the payor predeceases the annuitant, the fair market value of the property will be included in the estate and his executor will be allowed a deduction for the present value of future payments. For example, if Buck dies at the end of the tenth year, $100,000 (or whatever the market value is at that time) will be included in his estate. The present value of the annuity at Cash's age eighty would be 4.5164 multiplied by the annual payment $14,530 or a total of $65,623. This is the amount that could be deducted on the estate tax return.

The payor's estate would be confronted with two problems. First, taxes and other estate settlement costs would be increased due to inclusion of the property, and second, the estate would have to continue payments to the annuitant. This could create severe hardships for the payor's family. In order to protect against this contingency, the payor would probably be wise to acquire life insurance to offset the additional burdens against his estate.

CONCLUSION

Private annuities offer an excellent opportunity to transfer assets out of relatively high estate tax brackets; however, they require careful consideration by a qualified estate planning attorney before implementation. The tax consequences to all parties must be analyzed and all alternatives considered. The estate tax advantages are often offset by the income tax disadvantages.

CHAPTER XVIII

PURCHASE AND SALE AGREEMENTS

Buy-sell agreements in business situations can assure a market for a deceased business owner's interest and guarantee its value for tax purposes. These agreements fall into two basic categories: cross-purchase and entity. The cross-purchase agreement is one in which one partner or stockholder agrees to purchase the interest of another partner or stockholder upon that person's death, disability, or retirement. The entity agreement is one in which the partnership or corporation itself agrees to purchase the interest of the deceased, disabled, or retired person. A corporate entity buy-sell agreement is called a stock redemption agreement.

Selection of the proper form of agreement for each situation involves considerations such as: What is the best source of funds for payment? How many parties will participate in the agreement? Will payment be made in a lump sum or in installments? What are the tax ramifications of the agreement? When a business owner is considering buy-sell agreements, he should make certain his attorney is knowledgeable in both business law and taxation.

SURVIVING PARTNER OR STOCKHOLDER'S BASIS

One of the primary considerations in selecting between an entity and a cross-purchase agreement is the survivor's cost basis in the business. Under a cross-purchase agreement the survivor's cost basis is his original investment plus what he pays for the terminating party's interest. Under the entity plan, his basis is his original investment. Let's assume Jackie and Jill own a successful beauty school. When they started in business, ten years ago, they each invested $20,000. Today the business is worth at least $200,000. Each is willing to pay the other $100,000 for her interest in the business. Let's examine the cost basis consequences of each approach if Jill should die:

> **Cross-Purchase Agreement**—Jackie had originally invested $20,000 in the business. Since she is now purchasing Jill's share for $100,000, her basis for capital gain purposes is $120,000. If she were to sell to a large school for $200,000, she would realize a taxable gain of $80,000.
>
> **Entity Agreement**—Jackie had originally invested $20,000 in the business. The business itself purchases Jill's share for $100,000. Even though Jackie is now the sole owner of that business, her basis remains $20,000. If she were to sell for $200,000, she would realize a taxable gain of $180,000. If the capital gain consequences were the only consideration, the cross-purchase agreement would be used exclusively. We would not even have to discuss the entity approach.

HOW DOES THE SURVIVOR PAY FOR THE TERMINATED PARTNER'S INTEREST?

The source of funds for payment may have a bearing on which type of agreement is used. Let's assume first that the agreement will provide for installment payments. In a partnership, the situation will be approximately the same whether a cross-purchase or entity arrangement is used.

Essentially the survivor will have to use after tax dollars to make the payments; however, a part of each payment may be deductible by the partnership and taxable as ordinary income to the terminated partner or his family. There are some possible income tax advantages to the survivor and disadvantages to the terminated partner which are beyond the scope of this book. Each partner who is planning to enter into a buy-sell agreement should consider having independent counsel to make certain he is aware of the agreement's tax ramifications.

An installment buy-out in a corporate situation also requires the use of after tax dollars in making payments.

> **Example:** Tom, Dick, and Harry are equal owners in the TDH Corporation. The business is worth $1,200,000 and each of the three has been taking a salary of $60,000. The corporation has been taxed on another $100,000 in each of the last three years. They have a cross-purchase agreement which provides for a ten-year buy-out with interest at 8%. Let's assume that Tom dies. Dick and Harry will have to pay Tom's widow $40,000 of principal and $32,000 of interest during the first year.
>
> A replacement will have to be hired for Tom who has been acting as controller. It is estimated that replacement will cost approximately $30,000 per year. Their accountant and attorney tell them they cannot justify higher salaries; consequently they may have to declare dividends in order to get the money to pay Tom's widow. This would result in double taxation. There is a possibility they could borrow funds from the corporation, but their attorney cautions them the IRS may attempt to treat those loans as dividends.
>
> To illustrate the problem, let's assume all of the

after tax earnings are paid out in dividends. Prior to Tom's death, the corporation had pre-tax earnings of $100,000. Tom had received a salary of $60,000 and his replacement is receiving $30,000; consequently pre-tax earnings should increase to $130,000 (assuming no increase or decrease in operating profits). After state and federal taxes, there would be approximately $70,000 available for dividends.

The following illustration assumes Dick and Harry are currently in a combined state and federal tax bracket of 50% and that the dividends will be taxed at an average rate of 60%.

Payment		$40,000
Dividends	$70,000	
Interest on loan	$32,000	
Taxable	38,000	
Income Tax	22,800	
Available for principal payment		$15,200
Deficit		$24,800

Dick and Harry would have to come up with $24,800 from other sources to make the principal payment.

On the other hand, if the corporation itself were buying the stock from Tom's family, double taxation would be avoided and there would be a surplus available to the corporation.

Gross corporate profits	$130,000
Interest on loan	32,000
Net taxable	98,000
Corp. tax—state and federal	41,000
Available for principal pmt.	57,000
Principal payment	40,000
Surplus	17,000

The net result is that an entity buy-out would have saved Dick and Harry 41,800 ($17,000 corp. surplus plus $24,800 deficit on cross purchase).

Obviously, whenever stockholders intend to pay a deceased partner's heirs on an installment basis, the current income tax consequences as well as the future capital gains consequences must be taken into consideration.

The deceased stockholder's family may be dependent upon the continued success of the business. If Dick and Harry fall on hard times, they may not be able to continue the payments. Under the cross-purchase arrangement, Tom's family could probably sue each of them personally and attach personal assets; however, under a stock redemption agreement, the family's sole claim would be against the corporation itself.

One significant advantage of installment purchase to the family of the deceased stockholder is that the capital gain on sale can be reported as installments are received. If the gain is substantial, the income tax savings incident to installment purchase may outweigh the risk related to continuing success of the business.

Installment purchase may be the only approach that makes sense to both the buyer and the seller; however, careful consideration should be given to the problems outlined before a final decision is reached. Perhaps an installment purchase agreement funded by life insurance would solve all of the problems. Let's look at life insurance as a funding medium.

LIFE INSURANCE

There are a number of advantages to funding a buy-sell agreement with life insurance. First, the insurance proceeds are not subject to estate taxation or income taxation.* Second, the survivors will not have the burden of a substantial debt hanging over their heads. Third, the family of the deceased business owner will not be dependent upon the continued success of the business or the financial stability of the surviving owners.

The shortcomings of the insurance approach are few; however, they are worthy of consideration. First, the premiums are not tax deductible; consequently they must be paid with after tax dollars. Second, in a cross-purchase arrangement, a younger owner may not be able to afford sufficient insurance to buy out an older shareholder's interest. Third, life insurance in a stock redemption agreement may be inequitable to larger stockholders. For example, a 60% stockholder indirectly pays 60% of the premium whereas a 10% stockholder only pays 10% of the premium. In effect, the majority stockholder is providing the majority of funds to buy out his own stock.

Let's look at the TDH Corporation and assume Tom, Dick, and Harry decide to buy life insurance to fund the buy-out. Each would need $400,000 of coverage. They decide on permanent insurance instead of term because they will have a continuing need for the coverage. Tom's premium is $16,000, Dick's is $14,000, and Harry's is $12,000. After the first year, about 90% of the premium goes into cash value.

If the corporation buys the insurance, its outlay will be $42,000 per year. After the first year, the cash value increases will be about $38,000; consequently the protection itself will only cost about $4,000 plus what could have been earned on the $38,000 going into cash values. If one of the stockholders were

*There is a possibility of income taxation under the *transfer for value rule,* if ownership of a policy is transferred to anyone other than a partnership in which the insured is a partner, a partner of the insured, or a corporation in which the insured is a stockholder or officer. At the same time there is a move afoot to exclude from this rule transfers to other shareholders in the corporation.

to die under these circumstances, the insurance proceeds would be received by the corporation tax free and used to purchase his stock. The family would have the full economic value of the business, but the survivors would still be stuck with a low cost basis for future capital gains.

Let's see how a cross-purchase agreement might work in this situation. Each of the stockholders would own a $200,000 policy on each of the other stockholders' lives. Tom would be responsible for premiums of $13,000, Dick $14,000, and Harry $15,000. They would have a difficult time paying these premiums with after tax dollars. Once again, the corporation's status as a separate, independent entity comes to their rescue. They can split-dollar the insurance with the corporation. The corporation can pay the annual increases in cash value and Tom, Dick, and Harry the balance of the premium. Their total personal outlay would average about $1,300 each per year. If Tom were to pass away, Dick and Harry would each receive $200,000 less the accumulated cash values with which to buy Tom's share.

Several things can be done to make certain the survivors receive enough proceeds to make payment in full. First, a term rider can be added to each policy which increases at the same rate as the cash values. This is fine in the early years of the contract but can get prohibitively expensive as the insureds increase in age. Second, they can buy about 20% more insurance than is needed to fund the buy-out. This will solve the problem for six or seven years, and if a participating policy is used paid-up additions can be purchased with the dividends which will continue to solve the problem for several more years. Finally, there is the new concept of adjustable life which enables the policyholder to increase periodically his coverage consistent with increases in the cost of living without evidence of insurability.

The advantages of an insured cross-purchase agreement, once again, are that it will provide the surviving stockholders with a step-up in basis for capital gains tax purpose and provide the funds to pay for that stock tax free.

I have heard some insurance men analogize this type of purchase with a loan. You are in effect guaranteeing the availability of a certain sum of capital at an indeterminable future date by paying interest at a rate of 3% or 4% instead of waiting until that date arrives and borrowing money at the prevailing rate which might be 8% to 10% or 12%. It makes sense to me to make the smaller payments while you know you can so you are not forced to make higher payments when times might not be as good.

LIFE INSURANCE AND INSTALLMENT PURCHASE

The best of all worlds, from a tax point of view, might be attained by insuring an installment purchase agreement. The one drawback to this approach is the lack of any guarantee that the beneficiary of the insurance proceeds will use those proceeds to make the payments. He might decide he needs a new building or more modern equipment and assume the additional income he will generate will make the payment. One of the purposes for insuring the agreement is to avoid this kind of risk. Can anything be done?

Many attorneys and life underwriters are suggesting the use of a trusteed buy-sell agreement in which the insurance proceeds are paid to an independent trustee, the trustee makes periodic payments to the decedent's family, and simultaneously releases stock to the purchaser. This guarantees that the insurance proceeds will be used for the purpose intended and allows the survivors to report the capital gain over a number of years.

> **Warning**—An improperly drawn agreement might result in constructive receipt of the proceeds by the heirs. They might be taxed immediately in view of the fact they are guaranteed of receiving those proceeds. Make certain your attorney is well versed in this area before proceeding.

NUMBER OF PARTNERS OR SHAREHOLDERS

The insured cross-purchase arrangement is fairly easy to implement if there are two or three owners; however, it becomes cumbersome if there are more than three. For example, if there are four stockholders or partners, it may be necessary to issue twelve policies. Each stockholder would own a policy on the other three. If there are seven owners, forty-two policies would have to be issued. Under an entity-type agreement, only one policy on each owner would be required.

Multiple policies may also be avoided if the insurance company will reflect ownership as tenants in common. One policy could be issued specifying the percentage interest of each owner. Even though the number of policies is reduced, there are still potential problems. For example, what happens if one of the owners refuses to pay his share of the premium? If the others chip in to pay his share, how are they compensated?

STOCK REDEMPTION AGREEMENTS

As mentioned earlier, a stock redemption agreement is an entity purchase agreement for a corporation. The primary concern of redeeming stockholders is the tax treatment of funds received from the corporation in redemption of the stock. Generally speaking, distribution in redemption of stock will be treated as dividends to the extent the corporation has earned surplus; however, there are several exceptions to this rule.

Section 303 Redemption—Internal Revenue Section 303 provides that a redemption will not be treated as a dividend if the amount redeemed does not exceed all death taxes plus funeral and administrative expenses allowable as deductions for federal estate tax purposes.

In order to qualify for this exception, the value of the closely held stock must exceed 50% of the decedent's adjusted gross estate. If the estate elects and qualifies for installment payments of taxes, the redemption can take place anytime prior to the end of the installment period.

Prior to the Tax Reform Act of 1976, redemptions under Section 303 qualified for a stepped-up basis to the date of death and avoided capital gain treatment. The carryover basis provisions of TRA 76 eliminated this advantage (except that gains on stock acquired before December 31, 1979, will be based on its value on that date).

Section 303 redemptions provided a means for the estate of a business owner to obtain cash from the corporation without seriously diluting the estate's interest in the corporation. Assume Mr. A owns 1,000 shares of XYZ stock and this represents 100% of the outstanding stock. If the corporation redeems 300 shares, his estate will own 700 shares; however, this still represents 100% ownership.

The attractiveness of this approach has been diluted inasmuch as capital gain taxes may have to be paid. One approach being suggested by some attorneys is to combine a 303 redemption with installment payment of taxes. This would normally result in less taxation inasmuch as gains would be spread over a number of years.

Complete Redemption of all Stock—If all of a decedent's stock is redeemed, it will not be treated as a dividend. Unfortunately, for a redemption to be a complete redemption, any stock owned *directly or indirectly* by a spouse, children, grandchildren, and parents must also be redeemed. There are a number of exceptions, exceptions to the exceptions, and exceptions to the exceptions to the exceptions; consequently a knowledgeable attorney should be engaged to determine if a particular stockholder qualifies.

Substantially Disproportionate Redemption—To qualify as a substantially disproportionate redemption, immediately after the redemption the estate must own less than 50% of the total combined voting power. The amount of voting stock owned by the estate must be less than 80% of the total stock outstanding immediately before redemption. Unfortunately, stock of other family members is attributed as belonging to the deceased shareholder as described in the previous paragraph.

There are other exceptions to the rule that redemptions will be treated as dividends; however, a complete discussion of this topic is beyond the scope of this book.

Stock redemptions are not as attractive as they once were; however, there are a number of situations where they can still be utilized. This is one of many areas of estate planning in which it is vital that you be represented by an attorney knowledgeable in both tax and corporate law.

DECISION BETWEEN ENTITY AND CROSS-PURCHASE

The decision as to use of the entity or cross-purchase approach requires an in depth analysis of the advantages and disadvantages in each. Your attorney and CPA should be included in the decision-making process as soon as possible. If you intend to fund the agreement with life insurance, your insurance man's ideas and opinions should also be solicited.

PEGGING THE VALUE FOR ESTATE TAX PURPOSES

A properly drawn agreement can establish the value of a business for federal estate tax purposes. This is normally a desirable benefit because it eliminates the risk of the IRS arbitrarily placing a high value on the business. It also enables the business owner to plan with greater certainty because the value of the business can be ascertained at any point.

The price established should be a reasonable price approximating the true market value of the business. In other words, it should be a price a willing buyer would pay to a willing seller in an *arm's-length* transaction in which neither is under any compulsion to buy or sell.

There are five basic approaches to establishing a price for a closely held company: book value, capitalization of earnings, good will + return on investment, appraisal, and fixed price. Let's examine the pros and cons of each approach.

Book Value—Book value is the net asset value reflected on the balance sheet. The value of these assets is not their market value. Assets are normally stated at their acquisition cost, less an allowance for depreciation. Inventory values will vary depending on whether goods sold are treated on a "first in-first out" (FIFO) basis or a "last in-first out" (LIFO) basis. Book value does not normally include "good will." Good accounting practice does not consider good will to be an asset unless that good will was purchased from a former owner. The agreement could require an adjustment of book value to market value. This would mean all assets would have to be valued as of the date of sale. If the business owners decide to use book value as the valuation approach, the agreement should carefully define what is meant by book value and what adjustments, if any, should be made to the balance-sheet value.

Capitalization of Earnings—When an investor considers a security he places considerable emphasis on the company's earning power. How does one calculate the present value of a closely held company's future earnings?

One approach is to multiply an average of several years' earnings by a multiplier known as the capitalization factor. A company may have windfall earnings or a non-recurring loss in a particular year which could distort the average. Unusual items of this type should be considered when arriving at an average. The capitalization factor is the reciprocal of the return an investor expects to receive on his investment. If he expects a 20% return, the capitalization factor would be 5 ($5 \times 20 = 100$). In order to get a 25% return, the capitalization factor would be 4 ($4 \times 25 = 100$). The selection of a capitalization factor for any particular business is at best an educated guess. The variables include the extent of risk, the company's management, financial condition, the economic climate, rate of return from other investments, etc. Whatever capitalization factor is selected, it should be reviewed regularly. The business may be a high risk endeavor today, but five years from now it may mature into a stable, growing business. Similar businesses may be commanding higher or lower multiples in the future. Regular review will help keep the value of the business reasonable.

Good Will and Return on Investments—This approach distinguishes between return on tangible assets and the going concern value of the business. Let's assume a reasonable return to expect from plant and equipment would be 10% and a reasonable return on good will would be 20%.

Book value of the ABC Company is $100,000. This is not reflective of the true value adjusted to today's market. Adjusted book value of the ABC Company is $200,000. The company earns $50,000—the sale price would be calculated as follows:

Adjusted book value		$200,000
Average net earnings	$50,000	
10% return on book value	20,000	
Earnings attributed to Good will	30,000	
Capitalized at 20% Multiply by 5	5	
Good will		150,000
Value of the ABC Company		$350,000

The above approach has all the problems of both the book value method and the capitalization method. If it is used, it must be reviewed regularly to guarantee the rates of return are consistent with the changing economy and upon date of sale book value will have to be adjusted to reflect true market value.

Appraisal Method—Under this approach, an appraiser is hired to arrive at a value. The agreement should specify what appraiser is to be used in order to avoid any disagreement at the time of death. There are two disadvantages of this approach, one minor, one significant. The minor disadvantage is the necessity for paying an appraiser's fee. Such fees are not cheap, but the expense assures a reasonable, objective evaluation of the business. The second disadvantage is the difficulty in planning the business owner's estate. The actual sale price cannot be determined until the death occurs.

Fixed Price—The business owners, under this arrangement, agree upon a fixed price, uncomplicated by formulas or appraisals, and recite that price in the agreement. As in the other approaches, this should be reviewed regularly to guarantee the price is still fair and reasonable to both parties. The fixed price approach has several advantages. First, the business owners themselves determine what they consider to be a fair price. Second, it avoids the ambiguities and uncertainties of the other approaches. Finally, the estate planning can be implemented with certainty because the value of the business is a known quantity. Many attorneys recommend a protective provision in the event the purchase price is not redetermined regularly. For example, if the agreement provides for annual review and such review is overlooked, a provision could be included which after thirty, sixty, or ninety days requires the price to be determined by an alternate method. Of the above five approaches, the fixed price approach is the one favored by most estate planning specialists. If the price is reasonable and the business owners review it regularly, it will normally be accepted by the IRS for estate tax purposes. This is a significant advantage in estate planning, particularly where the business includes several members of the same family.

CONCLUSION

Buy-sell agreements are extremely useful in planning for the estate of closely held business owners. The decision, as to what type of agreement would be most beneficial, involves analysis of tax consequences, determination of how the agreement is to be funded, and the ultimate result each owner wants to accomplish. A properly drawn agreement can establish the value for estate tax purposes and enable the estate planner to plan with some degree of certainty as to his results.

PART IV

ESTATE PLANNING CASE STUDIES

CHAPTER XIX

ESTATE PLANNING FOR THE ELDERLY RETIRED

There are 21,000,000 individuals over age sixty-five in the United States. Every day 3,700 more reach this magic age of retirement. Most Americans, while waiting for that day to occur, dream of the financial and personal independence that are *supposed* to go with retirement. Those who are fortunate enough to realize their dreams often find that financial independence and personal freedom do not necessarily provide peace of mind. Let's look at a few typical cases.

THE SECOND MARRIAGE

Many lonely widows and widowers are unwilling to spend the rest of their lives alone; consequently we find a large number of second marriages among the elderly. Sonny and Happy Daze are just such a couple. Their first spouses died ten years ago. After a period of time they both sought companionship. Sonny and Happy met one afternoon over a bridge table and it was love at first sight. They have now been married for several years and are completely devoted to one another.

In the beginning, their children were surprised and shocked. It was difficult for them to accept their parents' need for love and companionship. But today the children of each marriage accept their step-parent as a family member and everybody is happy.

Neither Sonny nor Happy is what you would call a wealthy person, but each has a comfortable amount of assets. Sonny has property in his name with a value of about $150,000. Happy has assets in her name worth approximately $100,000. In addition, they have $20,000 in joint tenancy bank accounts and a condominium in joint names worth $50,000. Their combined estates would be worth $320,000.

Sonny's present will, written before his present marriage, leaves his estate to his children. Happy, at Sonny's suggestion, had a will drawn subsequent to the marriage leaving her estate to her children.

A few weeks ago, Sonny met with the trust officer at his bank who pointed out that the joint tenancy property would pass automatically to the survivor. He also advised Sonny to contact his attorney to review his will because under the laws of their state a will written prior to marriage might be invalid as to his spouse. This might result in one-third of the estate going outright to Happy and only two-thirds to the children.

As a result of that meeting, Sonny and Happy discussed their affairs and decided to revise their plans to provide more protection for the survivor. Sonny's initial idea was for each to leave everything to the survivor with the understanding the survivor would divide the entire estate equally among the children of both marriages.

Admittedly this was a simple plan which would accomplish their objectives; however, it was fraught with problems:

1. The estate would be subjected to unnecessary state and federal death taxes of approximately $50,000 upon the survivor's death.
2. The survivor might change his or her will, omitting one or more of the children. This is particularly likely if the children of the deceased spouse do not remain in close contact.
3. The survivor might transfer some of the assets into

joint tenancy with a child or a new spouse inadvertently thwarting the estate plan.

The attorney suggested a better approach might be to divide the assets as closely down the middle as they can, without incurring a gift tax. This would require elimination of all joint tenancies except a small bank account which could be kept for emergencies. Each will would create a trust, leaving the income to the survivor and directing that the principal go to the first decedent's children upon his or her death. Sonny's will would give Happy an income for life. If, for any reason, Happy is in need of additional funds, the trustee could use principal for her benefit. Upon Happy's death, Sonny's trust distributes outright to his children and Happy's estate distributes outright to her children. This approach would treat all of the children equitably and avoid approximately $50,000 of unnecessary death taxes.

THE CONCERNED SEPTUAGENERIAN

Annie Aware is a seventy-seven-year-old widow living in a retirement community. Over the last few years she has seen friends who were intelligent and alert one day and confused and disoriented the next day. She has seen others deteriorate so slowly that the process went unrecognized by family members and friends. Many people in various stages of senility are taken advantage of by financial scavengers, well-meaning friends, or greedy relatives. Annie wants to protect herself and her family from the dangers incident to her own possible senility.

Annie has an estate of approximately $200,000, consisting primarily of listed securities. She wants to continue making investment decisions while she is capable and would like to have her assets go to her children when she passes away. Annie's attorney informs her there are three alternatives from which she can choose: *conservatorship,* in which she names a third party as her conservator; *a living trust* in which she acts as her own trustee; and *a living trust* in which she hires a third party as trustee. The attorney discussed each approach with her in detail.

Conservatorship—Annie can nominate someone to act as conservator of her estate. She can ask that individual to serve now or at some unspecified later date when she is either incompetent or unwilling to continue managing her own affairs. Conservatorships are subject to court jurisdiction. The conservator would have to account to the court periodically, necessitating attorney fees and court costs. If Annie intends to have an individual handle her affairs, a conservatorship might be preferable because it would help to protect her from malfeasance and mismanagement. On the other hand, if she wants a corporate fiduciary to act, the living trust might be preferable.

Living Trust in Which Annie Is Her Own Trustee—A living trust with Annie as her own trustee could avoid probate if the assets are transferred properly and adequate records maintained. She would incur very little cost other than attorney fees for establishing the trust and additional accounting services. Annie could continue to manage her investments while she is mentally capable and turn over management to a successor when she no longer feels capable. Annie knows that she may not realize when she is starting to fail and that senility might creep up so slowly that those around her will not notice the change. Her attorney indicates another problem might exist if she is negligent in her record keeping. The successor trustee might have to charge a substantial fee to reconstruct her records, thereby reducing whatever savings might be realized from her acting as her own trustee.

Living Trust in Which Annie Has Her Bank As Trustee—This plan proved to be the one Annie preferred. While she is required to pay a fee now, at a time when she is fully capable of managing her own affairs, it seemed like a small premium to pay to guarantee protection for her family. Annie will continue to direct investment changes while she is capable; the bank will maintain all of her records, collect dividends, clip coupons, and so forth. A corollary advantage Annie had not previously considered is her freedom to travel extensively without having to worry about dividend checks, overdue coupons, or exercising warrants and rights.

The Loving Couple—S. O. and Vera Good have been married for sixty beautiful years. S. O., owner and president of a department store in the midwest, was a knowledgeable investor and an excellent provider for his family. About fifteen years ago S.O. retired and moved to California. Over the last few years Vera has noticed that S.O. is no longer as sharp as he used to be. He finds it difficult to balance his checkbook and becomes confused when confronted with relatively simple investment decisions. Vera has never made financial decisions and is not sure that S.O. would be able to adjust to her taking over. Not only that, but what if she is failing, too?

Vera consulted with her son, Charles, who had assumed presidency of the store when his father retired. Charles suggested she discuss the possibility of a trust with their attorney. In fact, he agreed to fly out for the meeting so that he could help convince S.O. of the desirability of a trust. An appointment was arranged for the following week.

While these arrangements were going on, S.O, who had recognized he was failing, was giving a lot of thought to how Vera would fare if he were to pass away. His will provided for marital and residual trusts in the event of his death, but Vera was named executrix and Charles and Vera co-trustees. S.O. was not sure Vera would be able to cope with the details and decisions of probate. He wanted her to be well provided for but unburdened with management.

The timing for the meeting with their attorney was perfect. The attorney agreed with Charles that a living trust would relieve his parents from the burdens of management. S.O. wanted Charles to be the trustee; however, Charles convinced his father it would be preferable to have someone nearby act. The attorney suggested the local bank which had a fine trust department, but this did not apeal to S.O. He felt the bank might be too impersonal, particularly when it came to providing for Vera. As an alternative, S.O. suggested they name Charles *and* the local bank co-trustees.

Once the technical aspects had been dealt with, S.O. and Vera were able to direct attention to the problems bothering them the most: who will make certain their personal needs are taken care of when and if they are no longer able to care for themselves. The absence of immediate family in the area is a drawback and Charles could not do it by long distance. A last resort would be to take them back to the midwest. Vera and S.O. are happy in California and would prefer to spend the rest of their lives in their new home.

The attorney suggests the problem may not be as serious as it appears. There are a great many retired people who welcome opportunities to act as companions or housekeepers. As long as the bank is handling the finances, a companion of this type could see to their personal needs. Perhaps they could test a few now, on a part-time basis. Even though a companion is not needed at this time, it would give S.O. and Vera a chance to select someone with whom they would be compatible.

All in all, Vera and S.O. were pleased with the meeting. —S.O. because Vera will be protected when he passes away and Vera because S.O. was willing to turn management over to Charles and the bank.

THE ELDERLY SINGLE

Ione Alone, age seventy-five, a retired spinster schoolteacher, is concerned that her modest estate will not last the rest of her life. She currently has $50,000 in savings accounts but has been depleting those accounts by $2,000 to

$3,000 a year during each of the last five years.

One of her neighbors, I. N. Sure, a retired life insurance executive, suggested she consider an annuity. He explained how it could be designed to provide her with an income for as long as she lives. She was receptive to the idea, so Mr. Sure asked a young man from his company, Mr. E. Z. Sales, to visit with her and describe some of the plans to her. Mr. Sales indicated there were two basic types of annuities which she might want to consider: fixed annuities and variable annuities. He explained that a fixed annuity would guarantee Miss Alone a fixed income for life. In addition to the guaranteed income, Miss Alone would participate in excess interest earned by the company. If she were to invest $40,000 in a fixed annuity today, she would receive $422.80 per month for the rest of her life.*

A variable annuity also contains a guarantee; however, that guarantee is less than under a fixed annuity. A portion of a variable annuity is invested in common stocks; this enables the annuitant to participate in the potential growth. At the present time, an investment of $40,000 in a variable annuity would generate $397.60 per month.* Part of this payment is guaranteed; however, the total payment would vary from year to year.

Miss Alone liked the idea of having a guaranteed income so she could not outlive her money. The variable annuity frightened her, but she recognized its potential as a hedge against future inflation. Miss Alone decided to invest $30,000 of her funds in a fixed annuity, $10,000 in a variable annuity, and retain $10,000 to meet emergencies and cover the cost of a few trips she plans to take.

CONCLUSION

Most retired people recognize the importance of estate planning to save taxes and protect their loved ones. Many of them,

*Non-refund annuities issued by a major insurance company for a female age 75 in 1978.

however, do not recognize the necessity for protecting themselves from the dangers of senility or the helplessness of ill health. An estate plan for an elderly person is only complete when it contains protection in the event of mental or physical disability.

CHAPTER XX

ESTATE PLANNING FOR THE PROFESSIONAL PERSON

Life is short and the art is long.—Hippocrates

Physicians and dentists usually get initiated into estate planning early in their careers, thanks to the persistence of thousands of life insurance agents who recognize them as good prospects. Attorneys and CPAs, on the other hand, do not have the immediate earning capacity of physicians and dentists and are not as universally successful. When they do become successful, it is difficult for anyone to approach them concerning their own planning. Many attorneys pass away without wills, or with estate plans so far outdated they are unworkable.

There are certain characteristics typical of most professionals which should be reviewed before we explore specific situations. First, most professionals start their careers heavily in debt and stay that way for a long time. Physicians and dentists have equipment to purchase. Attorneys need libraries and specialized publications. Many have obtained educational loans which must be paid off. As their earnings increase, they tend to go further and further in debt to improve their standards of living by continually acquiring new and bigger homes and cars.

Successful professionals earn substantial incomes. Most are in the top 5% of all incomes earned in the United States. Their incomes should remain at high levels through their entire careers unless interrupted by an unfortunate disability. Becoming accustomed to high income levels often makes it difficult for senior practitioners to retire. While they earn substantial incomes, very few accumulate enough assets to retire comfortably.

The primary asset of most professionals is life insurance. The balance of their investable funds goes into securities, real estate, and commercial tax shelters. Unfortunately, a majority of professionals, particularly physicians and dentists, have become victims of beautifully packaged, get-rich schemes, most of which have failed. In most instances, they would have been far better off turning their investments over to reputable professional investment advisors and allowing them to invest the funds conservatively.

Upon death, we are confronted with some problems peculiar to professional practices. How does one dispose of the practice? What steps must be taken to value accounts receivable? How do we go about collecting on them? What should be done to protect and dispose of confidential records? How do we value libraries, equipment, medicines, and so forth? To whom will these assets be sold? As you can see, there are a great many unique problems to consider in administering a professional person's estate.

Now, let's explore three types of situations: the sole practitioner, the partnership practice, and the professional corporation.

THE SOLE PRACTITIONER

Doctor I. Pullum is a successful forty-year-old dentist. He is married and has three teenage children. Last year he netted $50,000 after all business expenses and expects to do slightly better this year. Dr. Pullum has the following assets and liabilities:

		Monthly Payment	
Assets:			
Cash in the bank	$10,000		
Life insurance	150,000		
Accounts receivable (full value)	20,000		
Equipment (depreciated value)	10,000		
Residence	100,000		
Tax shelters (cost)	20,000		
Mountain condominium (½ interest)	25,000		
Automobiles and personal effects	25,000		
Total assets			$360,000
Liabilities:			
Life insurance loan	$5,000		
Mortgage on residence	65,000	$650	
Bank loan (used to acquire tax shelters) demand	15,000		
Mortgage on mountain condominium	15,000	150	
Auto loan	7,000	200	
Miscellaneous debts	3,000		
		$1,000	110,000
Net worth			$250,000

Several problems can be identified by analyzing these assets. First, the accounts receivable, equipment, and tax shelters would probably be discounted substantially if they were liquidated. Let's assume, after all collection costs, the receivables would net $16,000. Receivables are income in respect of decedent and would be taxed to the estate at ordinary income rates; consequently there will be some additional shrinkage due to those taxes. The equipment will have to be appraised and then sold to a new dentist. Perhaps we could net $8,000 from the sale of this equipment. The tax shelters are not liquid and it is impossible to sell them at this time. Available information indicates we might receive up to $8,000 over the next three years. The total death value of these assets would be $30,000 instead of $50,000 reducing the net worth to $230,000.

It may be possible to find a buyer for Dr. Pullum's entire practice; however, this is unusual unless an agreement is entered into in advance; consequently the doctor's confidential records must be preserved until called for by a patient's new dentist. Some associations may be willing to hold those records; however, if they are not, the executor or trustee may have to hold them until they are called for. An alternative solution might be for Dr. Pullum to name another dentist as trustee of those records under his will.

Valuation of the equipment and location of a purchaser can pose problems; however, many equipment suppliers will help in the valuation and locate potential buyers. Another source of potential buyers is the graduating class at a nearby dental school.

The only potential income producing asset in Dr. Pullum's estate is his life insurance. His family will net $145,000 from the insurance ($150,000 face amount less the $5,000 loan). Assuming a 7% return, the insurance will generate approximately $850 per month. The accounts receivable and proceeds of sale of the equipment, as well as the cash in the bank, would probably be eaten up in estate settlement costs, repaying the bank loan, and paying off the miscellaneous debts.

Mrs. Pullum might also have social security available. Let's assume this will generate an additional $750 per month so that her total income is $1,600 per month. The installment loan payments total $1,000 per month; consequently only $600 per month would be available to cover food, clothing, medical expenses, education, insurance, taxes, and other costs of maintaining the household. In addition, social security will only be available until the youngest child either attains age eighteen or age twenty-two if he is in college. In any event, it will decrease as the children reach majority. Obviously Dr. Pullum needs additional life insurance.

The house and condominium loans could be paid off. This would decrease Mrs. Pullum's income by $467 a month, but would decrease her payments by $800, thereby increasing her spendable income to $933 per month. For our purposes, we should assume there will always be automobile payments; therefore that loan should not be repaid.

How much additional life insurance should Dr. Pullum acquire? That depends entirely on how much income Mrs. Pullum will need to maintain her living style and whether he wants her to use principal as well as income to satisfy that need. Let's assume that after reviewing the family budget, they decide another $700 of income is the minimum she can get by on. Based on our earlier assumption of a 7% return, Dr. Pullum should acquire an additional $120,000 of life insurance. Some people may want to consider potential inflation and provide for additional coverage. My personal preference is to plan for today and assume the current and future investment programs will offset inflation.

Dr. Pullum will probably say, "I can't afford more life insurance," but he can't afford not to acquire more life insurance. If he considers it as a savings medium it may be more palatable. Permanent insurance is one way to force yourself to develop a liquid reserve.

Perhaps we can suggest a way to acquire the insurance using pre-tax dollars. The doctor could establish a Keogh plan with his insurance company and acquire the insurance through that plan. In effect, the cash value increases will be tax deductible.

He can contribute 15% of his income up to $7,500 of pre-tax dollars each year. Since he is probably in a 50% income tax bracket, the real cost of this contribution is $3,750.

The only drawback to this approach is the fact he will have to include his office staff in the plan. The cost of providing for them must be taken into consideration before making a decision.

At Dr. Pullum's age, the premium for ordinary life would be approximately one-half the annual contribution; consequently the remaining $3,750 could be invested to yield a significant return. Under a typical plan,* assuming the investment yields 7%, Dr. Pullum at age sixty-five would have cash values and dividends approximating $157,000 and $237,000 in the investment account for a total of $394,000. If he dies his family is adequately provided for, and if he lives he will have a substantial retirement income.

Dr. Pullum should consider either a testamentary trust or a revocable life insurance trust to receive the proceeds of his insurance and his Keogh plan. The tax savings on Mrs. Pullum's second death will be substantial and the trustee can provide the management necessary to obtain maximum value from the insurance proceeds. The accounts receivable should probably be directed to the residual trust in order to obtain the estate tax deduction attributable to income in respect of decedent. This deduction may be lost if those receivables are paid to his widow or the marital deduction trust.

The proceeds of the Keogh plan can either be paid to the trust or in a lump sum or paid out to the trust or the widow in the form of an annuity. If payable in a lump sum the proceeds will be subject to estate tax and qualify for a special income-averaging provision for income tax purposes. If payable in the form of an annuity, the proceeds are exempt from estate taxation but taxable to the beneficiary at ordinary income tax rates. If desired, the proceeds can be paid out over as short a period

*A major insurance company's—whole life policy—non-smoker rates using 1976 dividend scale.

as thirty-six months and still be exempt from estate taxation. Each individual's circumstances must be reviewed carefully to determine the most favorable manner in which payments should be made.

As you can see, the sole practitioner's estate presents some interesting opportunities for planning; however, the problems relating to disposition of business assets are quite complex. You will see how this type of problem can be more easily solved in the partnership or professional corporation.

THE PARTNERSHIP PRACTICE

The firm of Good and Legal has been practicing as a partnership for many years. Ms. Sue M. Good at age fifty-five is the senior partner. I. L. Legal, who is about fifty, joined forces with her about ten years ago. They have two young men who came with the firm three years ago and who will become partners this year.

One of the big advantages of a partnership over a solo practice is the fact that there is a logical market for a deceased partner's interest in the practice. The surviving partners are more than willing to participate in the purchase.

Not only is there a ready market, but a continuing practice contains an element of good will which does not exist in an individual practice. The value of this good will increases the value of the deceased partner's estate.

It is important to have a formal written buy-sell agreement, binding the surviving partners to purchase the deceased partner's interest at a predetermined price. A well-drafted agreement can establish a value acceptable by the IRS for estate tax purposes.

Ms. Good and Mr. Legal have had such an agreement for several years. A value of $400,000 had been placed on the partnership indicating that each partner's interest is worth $200,000. As soon as the new partners are admitted, the value will be increased to $600,000 with one-third attributed to Ms. Good, one-third to Mr. Legal, and one-sixth to each of the new partners. The agreement can be funded or unfunded. That is, insurance can be acquired to purchase a deceased partner's interest or the partnership can pay for it out of future income. The agreement can provide for either a lump sum payment or installment payments. The agreement should define what portion of the payment constitutes good will, accounts receivable, and other future income and physical assets.

The portion of the payment representing physical assets and good will is taxable as capital gain to the estate and the part attributable to income will be treated as ordinary income. If payment is made in a lump sum, all of the ordinary income and capital gains will be taxed in one year. If it is paid in installments, the tax will be spread over the installment period.

The firm of Good & Legal owns its own building worth $150,000, furniture and equipment worth $50,000, and accounts receivable totaling $50,000. The balance of the value ($350,000) is the firm's good will. Capital accounts reflect a total investment of $100,000. If Ms. Good were to die, her interest in the partnership would be valued at $200,000. Her share of the capital account is $50,000; consequently her heirs would pay income taxes (ordinary and capital gain) on $150,000, broken down as follows:

Ordinary income (1/3 of accounts receivable):	$16,666.67
Capital gain:	133,333.33
Total Taxable:	$150,000.00

If paid in a lump sum, the capital gain would be taxed at the maximum rate and also be subject to the minimum tax on preference items.

If the partners want to assure that payment will be made regardless of the continued success of the practice, the agreement should probably be funded. It is not necessary, however, for the proceeds of the insurance to be paid out in a lump sum. The buy-sell agreement can be trusteed. A trustee can be named to receive the proceeds and pay them out in periodic installments as provided in the agreement. This will guarantee the deceased partner's estate of receiving all it is entitled to at the lowest possible tax rates. Good and Legal have insured all parties and named the Barrister Trust Company to receive the proceeds and pay those proceeds to the heirs in ten equal installments.

Inasmuch as the cost of insurance is greater the older you become, younger partners may have difficulty paying premiums on older partners' lives. On the other hand, the probability that they will benefit is greater than that of the older partners. While cross-ownership is the most equitable approach, many partnerships, as an entity, acquire the insurance on each of the partners and allocate premiums equally. This is inequitable to the older partners because they are paying for part of the insurance on their own lives, but they are usually willing to assume that cost to guarantee that their families will receive full value.

Ms. Good and Mr. Legal acquired their insurance when they were considerably younger, therefore it had accumulated significant cash values when the new partners were admitted. Each of the new partners executed a note for his share of the cash value which is to be paid off over a five-year period. Because of the older policies, premiums for the younger partners and older partners are approximately equal. As soon as the notes are paid off, each will be paying roughly the same amount per thousand of coverage.

A partnership provides a ready buyer for the practice, but it does not provide many other estate planning opportunities beyond those available to the sole practitioner. The professional corporation on the other hand offers several unique planning opportunities.

THE PROFESSIONAL CORPORATION

About four years ago, Russ T. Needle, age fifty; Anna Stetic, age forty-five; and Seymore Butts, age forty-eight, converted their medical partnership into a professional corporation going under the name of Needle, Stetic and Butts, P.C. All three are highly successful and are taking salaries of $100,000 each. The professional corporation provides them with significant tax advantages they could not have obtained in the partnership.

First, they created a qualified retirement plan to which the corporation contributes $25,000 per year for each of them. Tax will be deferred on these funds until they are distributed to the doctors. Contributions to corporate plans are not subject to the same 15% or $7,500 restriction imposed on Keogh plans. They can total 25%, and sometimes more, of the doctor employee's salary. Assuming a 7% rate of return, the doctors would accumulate the following amounts by age sixty-five: Dr. Needle, $935,000; Dr. Stetic, $1,455,000; and Dr. Butts $1,121,000. As you can see, it is possible to accumulate a substantial estate solely through a conservatively invested qualified retirement plan.

Second, the corporation installed a group life insurance program, providing $50,000 of group term insurance for each doctor. The premiums for this insurance are deductible by the corporation. Additional amounts can be obtained, but a small cost factor will be taxable to the doctors as additional income.

Third, they instituted a group accident and health insurance plan and superimposed an excess medical reimbursement plan on top of it. The group insurance is deductible by the corporation and non-taxable to the doctors. The medical reimbursement plan provides that if they have medical expenses in excess of what is covered by the group plan, the corporation will pay the balance. Once again this is non-taxable to the doctors and deductible by the corporation.

Finally, they had the corporation establish a disability income plan that would replace their incomes if they become disabled. The plan is funded with disability income insurance on which the corporation pays and deducts the premium. When, and if, one of the doctors becomes disabled, the payments will be taxable to him as ordinary income. There is another school of thought which suggests that the doctors acquire disability income coverage personally instead of through the corporation. If they do acquire it personally, the premium is nondeductible, but the proceeds are tax free. The proponents of corporate-owned disability income claim a certain tax break today is better than a *possible* tax break in the future. Proponents of personally owned disability income argue, "Why take a small tax deduction now, when you can receive thousands tax free if you become disabled?" Either approach is viable. It is up to you to decide which you prefer.

Incorporation seems to work fine for Needle, Stetic and Butts, P.C., but it will not be practical in every instance. The income level at which a doctor should start considering incorporation is $50,000.

It cost Needle, Stetic and Butts, P.C., over $5,000 to get the corporation set up. Their annual accounting costs have increased another thousand. The employer's share of social security is costing them another $1,500 a year, and contributions to the retirement plan for their employees is costing them $15,000 per year. However, in the overall picture they are saving about $20,000 per year by being incorporated.

Upon the death of a stockholder, the surviving stockholders will usually purchase the deceased stockholders' shares from the estate. If they have a formal buy-sell agreement, the price will be determined in advance and the estate will be assured of a fair price. A properly drawn buy-sell agreement will also establish the value of the practice for federal estate tax purposes.

Dr. Stetic is married to an attorney who is also moderately successful. They have been able to accumulate a considerable estate outside of the professional corporation. The Stetics are currently providing $400 per month for the support of Dr. Stetic's mother. In addition, they have two children away from home at college. Both children plan to become physicians.

It would be advisable for the Stetics to consider irrevocable trusts. Either ten-year trusts with principal reverting to them or lifetime trusts could be used (See Chapter II.) Because of their tremendous earning capacity and accumulations within the corporation, it would appear that lifetime trusts would be preferable. If Dr. Stetic's mother dies, her share could augment the children's trusts.

If both spouses join in a gift of $70,000 to each trust, they should get by with little or no current federal tax and a small state tax. At a 7% rate this will remove $14,700 from their taxable incomes. This is investment income taxed in the 70% bracket; consequently there will be an increase in family spendable income of $10,290 reduced only by trustee's fees of approximately $1,500 and the income tax attributable to each beneficiary. Let's assume the total taxes would be another $1,500. The net savings would be $7,290 per year. Irrevocable trusts appear ideal in this situation.

Incorporation seems to work fine for Needle, Stetic and Butts, P.C.; however, it is not advisable for all professionals. Some will be emotionally unable to cope with the discipline required to make it work. Professionals should probably have incomes in excess of $50,000 before giving consideration to incorporation and should have a reputable CPA firm perform a feasibility study before any action is taken. Doctors and dentists are the most vulnerable of the professionals. It would be money well spent to engage the services of the best CPA and tax attorney in their community. If you need a referral from someone who knows the tax professionals well, ask the trust officer at your bank.

CHAPTER XXI

ESTATE PLANNING FOR THE BUSINESS OWNER

The small businessman's estate presents a distinct challenge to the estate planner. Quite often the business is the only income-producing asset and its ability to continue generating income after the owner's death is the focal point of the estate plan.

There are three basic forms of doing business: sole proprietorship, partnership, and incorporation. Some of the problems we discuss in the first two areas can be solved by incorporation; consequently I would encourage the sole proprietor or partner to read the segment on the corporate business owner.

Now, let's look at the problems confronting the sole proprietor and some possible solutions to those problems.

THE SOLE PROPRIETOR

The sole proprietor has a unique estate planning problem because when he dies the business often dies with him. Many businessmen elect this form of doing business because of its simplicity. The legal and tax problems confronting partnerships and corporations are avoided and the business owner can make decisions without accounting to boards of directors or obtaining approval of his partners.

When a sole proprietor dies, his business assets become part of his estate and his business liabilities become estate liabilities. If the proprietor's will does not contain a provision to the contrary, his personal representative must liquidate the business as soon as possible. The enterprise cannot be continued except to the extent necessary to complete any unfinished business.

In order to maximize the value of the business for the heirs, the personal representative will first attempt to sell the business as a going concern. It is not always possible to find a buyer quickly, and more often than not that buyer will take advantage of the circumstances and offer far less than the business is really worth.

If there is no buyer for the business as a going concern, the assets will be sold to the highest bidder. Usually the sale takes the form of a public auction. Merchandise will probably be sold to others in the same line of business; consequently it is unlikely they will pay anywhere near what they could acquire new merchandise for. Furniture and fixtures will be sold to second-hand dealers who will bid low enough to make a reasonable profit on resale. The estate will realize far less than the fair market value of the assets. All in all, a forced sale should be avoided if at all possible.

Sometimes the personal representative will attempt to continue the business for the benefit of the heirs. If he does so without authority he becomes personally liable for all business debts and is personally responsible to the beneficiaries for all losses. He can avoid responsibility for losses if all other beneficiaries agree to the continuation of the business; however, if any of the beneficiaries are minors, guardians would have to be appointed to provide approval for them.

The concerned sole proprietor should carefully consider the alternatives available to him and plan in advance for what will happen to his business in the event of his death. Does he want it retained by his family, does he want it sold to one or more employees, or does he want it liquidated? Whichever choice he makes, he should take whatever legal steps may be necessary to assure a quick and efficient transition.

Retention—Can the family continue to operate the business profitably? Several factors will help the business owner make this determination. The first and most important consideration is whether or not there would be capable successor management. If the owner believes an employee or family member could run the business, he should start training that individual immediately.

Profits will probably be reduced if it is necessary to add an additional employee to replace the owner. The business owner should calculate what the family may expect to net after all expenses including the new employee's salary.

If the business has been in the family for many years and has a loyal group of customers, the mere fact it is being retained by the family may keep it profitable.

One important consideration in retention is whether or not there is adequate liquidity available to cover estate settlement costs, debts, and taxes. One liquidity need which is not always considered is the need for cash to repay bank loans. While the bank might take care of all of the owner's financing needs during his lifetime, it may be reluctant to carry his heirs after his death.

If the owner decides to have the business retained, he should take several steps to guarantee the continued success of the business. First, his will should give his personal representative the power to retain the business, operate it, borrow, and reorganize, if necessary. Second, he should make certain there is adequate cash available to settle the estate, pay taxes and business debts, and continue the business. Most businessmen do not like to hold large amounts of liquid assets. They want their assets to be as productive as possible. The best way to assure availability of cash at death without tying up cash today is with life insurance. The business owner with foresight will acquire enough life insurance today to meet his future cash needs.

If the proprietor has several children, but only one child will be involved in the business, inequities could arise. It would be unfair for profits of the business to be divided among all family members if one particular individual is responsible for those profits. It would also be unfair to leave a fairly valuable business to one child and modest bequests of other assets to the other children.

Case Study—Mr. H.A. (Hab) Berdasher owns a clothing store which specializes in quality apparel for men. The business is very successful and is recognized as *the* place to buy clothes if you want to be in style. His son Tailor has worked with his father for five years and has been responsible for a continuing younger clientele. Tailor now supervises all sales activities and Hab does all the buying and handles all financial matters. The business generates a very comfortable living for Mr. Berdasher. He nets approximately $50,000 per year and the business has a net worth of about $150,000, taking into consideration $50,000 he owes the Second National Bank. He also owns the building in which the business is located and estimates it to have a value of $100,000. He has cash and securities worth $50,000, $100,000 of life insurance, and a $100,000 home which is free and clear, for a total estate of $500,000. Mr. Berdasher estimates his wife will need approximately $25,000 per year to maintain her present standard of living. In addition to his son, he has a twenty-four-year-old daughter, Sophie, who is unmarried and living at home. Sophie is currently studying for the ministry and does not anticipate a very substantial income. Hab's present will leaves the entire estate outright to Mrs. B. Upon her death, the estate is divided equally between the two children. There are no provisions relating to the continuation of the business. This estate plan poses six problems:

1. Approximately $80,000 in unnecessary taxes and settlement costs will be paid on the second death.
2. Specific authority will have to be obtained for Mrs. B to continue the business.

3. The Second National Bank will require repayment of the $50,000 loan since it was made against Hab's signature.
4. It will be necessary to hire one and possibly two people to assume Hab's duties. This may reduce the income below what is needed for Mrs. B to maintain her standard of living.
5. Tailor will still be an employee with no ownership, subject to his mother's orders. Mrs. B may take an active role in the business even though she has no experience.
6. The two children will become equal partners upon the death of the surviving parent.

Hab's attorney and CPA make several suggestions which will eliminate many of the problems in his estate.

1. Utilize marital deduction and family trusts to minimize taxes. The tax savings would amount to approximately $80,000. Mrs. B can receive all income from both trusts over her lifetime. Upon Mrs. B's death, Tailor's share would be distributed outright to him, but Sophie's would remain in trust for her lifetime to make certain she always has a dependable source of income.
2. Enter into a buy-sell agreement with Tailor so that he will have complete control of the business immediately after Hab's death.

   The building should be kept separate from the business assets and excluded from the buy-sell. This would reduce Tailor's purchase price and provide the trust with a good income-producing asset regardless of whether the business succeeds or fails. Tailor can rent the building from the trust for as long as he is in business; however, the rental terms should be consistent with what any other tenant would pay.

The buy-sell agreement could provide for Tailor to pay for the business over a period of years; however, an installment buy-out poses problems.

The payments have to be made with after tax dollars. If Tailor is in a 40% tax bracket and the principal payments are $10,000 per year, he will have to earn $16,667 in order to make those $10,000 payments. In addition, he will have to pay interest on the loan. Interest at the rate of 7% would require an additional $8,500 the first year. $25,167 of Tailor's first-year earnings would be required to make the loan payments.

If Tailor misses a payment, it could result in family dissension.

If Tailor misses several payments, the trustee would probably have to foreclose on him.

If it is necessary to hire a replacement for Mr. B, the business may not be able to generate, enough income to both pay his salary and make the loan payments. Tailor could consider acquiring some life insurance on Hab to provide working capital and/or cover the purchase price.

Fifty thousand dollars would cover the working capital, but the estate would still be dependent upon the continued success of the business.

One hundred fifty thousand dollars would cover the purchase price, assuming Hab was willing to sell to Tailor for the net asset value. Tailor could then pledge assets to obtain working capital. The estate would not be dependent upon the continued success of the business, and Mrs. B and Sophie would have a steady source of income independent of the business.

Hab could either increase Tailor's salary to provide him with enough income to pay the premiums, or split-dollar the insurance with him. In a split-dollar plan, Hab would pay an amount equal to the annual increases in cash value and Tailor would pay the balance of the premium. Upon Hab's death, the accumulated cash values would become part of his estate, and the balance of the insurance would go to Tailor to help him buy the business.

By implementing some of these suggestions, the administration of Hab's estate will be simplified and the continuation of the business by Tailor guaranteed.

Sale to Employees—Many sole proprietors have a great deal of affection for individuals who have been loyal and trusted employees. They would like those employees to be protected in the event of their deaths. If the business is liquidated, the employees will be out of a job. If it is sold to a new owner, he may want to hire his own people. A sale to one or more key employees may be the answer. The big problem is money to cover the purchase price. The buy-sell agreement could provide for the business to be paid for over a number of years. The primary disadvantage of this arrangement is that if the business fails, the heirs will suffer. The employees may be able to borrow part of the purchase price from the bank; however, this may put them in a cash bind as far as working capital is concerned. Once again, the ideal answer, if the proprietor qualifies, is life insurance. Employees' salaries could be increased to help offset the insurance cost and/or the proprietor could split-dollar the insurance with them. If the employer cannot qualify for life insurance, the employees could establish a sinking fund, into which they contribute a certain amount each month toward a future purchase. This is not an ideal solution but should help to provide part of the purchase price.

In situations where the proprietor has substantial assets outside of the business, he may want to set a relatively low purchase price for his employees. There is one possible problem with this approach. If the price is considerably below market value, the IRS might treat the sale as a partial bequest and tax it in the proprietor's estate. While this possibility does exist, the probability is remote if certain formalities are adhered to in the buy-sell agreement itself.

Liquidation—Many sole proprietors have little choice but to have the business liquidated upon their deaths. There may be no one in the family interested in the business and no employees capable of running it, or the nature of the business might be such that it is completely dependent upon the skills and contacts of the proprietor. His death leaves nothing to continue. Even in situations where liquidation is the only answer, some planning must be done. The proprietor's will should give his executor broad powers concerning when and how the business should be liquidated. The more discretion the executor has, the more likely he will maximize the proceeds from the sale. The proprietor should write a letter of instructions to his executor outlining what he believes to be the best way to maximize the return from liquidation. The letter should provide the names of individuals who might be interested in specific items. This type of information will save the executor time and, consequently, save the estate some money. When a business is liquidated, the income generated by that business ceases. The proprietor must accumulate other income-producing assets to provide for his family. Until he has accumulated enough assets to offset the loss of his earning power, he should consider acquiring sufficient life insurance to replace the lost income.

Conclusion—The sole proprietor must decide whether his business should be continued by the family, sold to employees, or liquidated. Once he makes this determination it is imperative for him to devise an estate plan which will protect his family and provide for an orderly business transition. Incorporation should also be considered for both lifetime tax savings and ease of transfer at death. Read on!

PARTNERSHIPS

Partnerships are divided into two primary categories: general and limited. A general partnership is one in which all of the partners are involved in the management of partnership assets and each partner is financially responsible for the actions of all other partners. A limited partnership has two classes of partners. The general partner manages the partnership assets and is solely responsible for the debts of the partnership. The liability of limited partners is limited to the extent of their investment in the enterprise. They lose the advantage of limited liability if they become involved in management at any time.

The general partnership is the one most commonly used to operate a business enterprise. Two or three individuals agree to pool their talents and resources and a partnership is formed. The compatibility of these individuals is probably the key ingredient in their success or failure, and herein lies the primary estate planning problem for partnerships.

If one partner dies, the surviving partners do not normally want to be in business with the deceased partner's widow or widower. They would prefer to seek out a new partner with talents similar to those of the deceased partner. The only way to accomplish this short of liquidation and reorganization after death is for the partners to enter into a buy-sell agreement.

The surviving partners would agree to pay the deceased partner a fair value for the business. The surviving spouse would not become an unwanted and possibly disruptive new business associate; however, that spouse would receive a realistic value for that business as agreed upon by the deceased partner.

Many partnerships have grown to the point where they should consider incorporation to obtain income tax savings, limit personal liability, and/or provide ease of transfer at death. Read on!

THE CORPORATE BUSINESS OWNER

The corporate business owner has a number of tools available to him that are not available to either the sole proprietor or partner. The first favorable estate planning characteristic of the corporation is limited liability. The sole proprietor and his estate are responsible for all existing and potential liabilities of the business. A partner's personal assets are on the line for liabilities of the partnership. But a corporate shareholder's liability can be limited to the assets of the corporation.

Another positive characteristic of the corporation is ease of transferring ownership. Ownership in the corporation is evidenced by stock certificates which can transfer ownership by the stroke of a pen. There is no need to execute a deed for each parcel of real property or transfer ownership of other individual assets.

Another advantage of the corporation is its acceptance as a separate entity. An owner may die but the corporation continues. This is true even if the sole stockholder dies. In addition the corporation can be treated as a separate taxpayer. This status as a taxable entity provides many opportunities to reduce the owner's over-all income taxes. Assume Mr. Pres I. Dent has a small unincorporated manufacturing company which generates $60,000 of taxable income. Mr. Dent pays $22,300 of taxes. He reinvests another $18,000 in the business, leaving him with $19,700 of spendable income. His accountant, I. M. Sharp, CPA, suggests he incorporate the business, pay himself a salary of $35,000, and leave $25,000 in the corporation. The tax on Mr. Dent's salary would be $9,920, leaving him $25,080 spendable (an increase of $5,380). The corporation's tax would be $5,500, leaving it with $19,500 for investment (an increase of $1,500). The total reduction in taxes for one year would be $6,880.

Caveat—Mr. Dent should not automatically run out and incorporate. The cost of incorporation, the necessity for paying corporate social security taxes on Mr. Dent's salary, and the fact that funds left in the corporation will be taxed again when, and if, distributed, may dampen his enthusiasm.

On the other hand, there are more potential advantages to consider:

1. Mr. Dent can set up a qualified retirement plan through the corporation. The payments to this plan are deductible by the corporation and accumulate tax free. Unfortunately he may have to include all of his employees. Payments for their benefit may offset the potential savings to Mr. Dent.
2. The corporation can deduct the cost of medical reimbursements to Mr. Dent over and above his group insurance costs as long as those payments are made subject to a plan formally adopted by the board of directors.
3. Up to $50,000 of group life insurance can be acquired on Mr. Dent's life and deductible by the corporation. Other employees must be included in the group life program.
4. A disability income plan can be established in which either the premiums for the coverage or the payments during disability are deductible.

The corporation can provide an ideal vehicle for estate planning. Mr. Dent can make annual gifts of corporate stock to his children, grandchildren, key employees, charities, or to whomever he deems appropriate. While he continues to own at least 51% of the stock, he effectively controls the destiny of his corporation.

The corporation can acquire life insurance on Mr. Dent's life. Recent cases have held that the value of his stock will only be increased by a portion of the insurance equivalent to his stock ownership. For example, assume the corporation is worth $500,000 and Mr. Dent owns 60% of the stock. His interest in the corporation prior to his death is worth $300,000. If the corporation owns $100,000 of life insurance on Mr. Dent's life, the value of his stock would be increased by $60,000 (60% of $100,000). The remaining $40,000 of insurance proceeds would be completely tax free.

If the corporation is continued after Mr. Dent's death, careful consideration needs to be given as to how to get income to various family members. It cannot legitimately be paid out in the form of salaries unless the family members are providing services to the corporation. If it is necessary to pay income out in the form of dividends, those dividends will be taxed twice: first to the corporation and second to the recipient.

One possible solution is for Mr. Dent to enter into a deferred compensation agreement with his company which would guarantee an income to him if he retires and, more importantly, guarantee a reasonable income to his wife if he should pass away. Under this plan, the corporation could deduct the payments and avoid double taxation on its income. Also, the payments would continue even if the corporation were sold.

Minority Stockholders—Deferred compensation plans are particularly desirable in the case of minority stockholders. Families of minority stockholders are extremely vulnerable. They are not likely to get hired as employees and it is virtually impossible to get majority stockholders to pay dividends. If the family decides to sell their interest in the corporation, they will find no market for their stock. They are completely at the mercy of the majority stockholders. Perhaps the best answer available to the minority stockholder or the majority stockholder whose family would be unable to manage the business would be to enter into a buy-sell agreement. This arrangement provides the family with reasonable compensation for the deceased stockholder's interest and enables the surviving stockholders to run the business without the interference or annoyance which might be caused by the deceased stockholder's heirs.

CONCLUSION

Planning for the business owner requires intimate knowledge of the business itself as well as the needs of the business owner's family. Some of the problems and solutions have been covered in this chapter; however, complete treatment of this subject is beyond the scope of this book. I would encourage any business owner to engage the services of a competent tax attorney, a qualified CPA, and a reputable insurance man to assist in planning for the continuity or disposition of the business.

CHAPTER XXII

ESTATE PLANNING FOR THE CORPORATE EXECUTIVE

Corporate executives have a great many fringe benefits which make up the majority of their estates. Take the case of Mr. Typical Veep, age forty-five. Mr. Veep is Executive V.P. of Hops United Grape Exporters (HUGE). He earns $60,000 per year. For many years HUGE had problems retaining top executives. Then, a few years back, they hired an executive compensation firm to develop a compensation package that would tie their top executives to them. The primary assets in Mr. Veep's estate are a result of this package.

Mr. Veep owns 36,000 shares of HUGE which he has acquired under a very favorable loan program. This stock is currently worth $720,000 and he owes $400,000 on which he pays interest only each year of $20,000. The stock pays $18,000 in dividends; consequently his out-of-pocket cost to acquire the stock is only $2,000 per year.

The company has a basic group life insurance plan which provides $50,000 of free insurance. In addition Mr. Veep has the right to purchase up to two times that amount at extremely favorable rates. He has exercised that right and now has $150,000 of group life insurance.

HUGE's pension plan will pay Mr. Veep an income of

$30,000 per year commencing at age sixty-five. There is no provision for any death benefit to Mrs. Veep if Typical should pass away prior to attaining age sixty-five; however, if he dies after retirement a reduced pension of $15,000 will be paid to her for life.

The company's profit sharing plan has been in existence for five years. Mr. Veep's interest is worth about $30,000 and he is 50% vested. That means, if he were to leave today, he would be entitled to one-half of the amount in his profit sharing account ($15,000).

Mr. and Mrs. Veep own their home, valued at $250,000, in Denver's fashionable Cherry Hills area. I should say the bank owns it to the extent of $150,000 and they allow the Veeps to live there as long as they continue to make their $1,500 monthly payments.

Their furniture, furnishings, jewelry, and automobiles are valued at $50,000 and they owe $12,000 on the automobiles.

The checking account seldom contains more than $2,000 and they have a $5,000 savings account which has been set aside for their son's education.

Let's look at the Veeps' balance sheet.

Assets		*Liabilities*	
HUGE stock	$720,000	Stock loan	$400,000
Vested int. in PS	15,000	R.E.Mortgage	150,000
Residence	250,000	Car loans	12,000
Furn., etc.	50,000		
Cash	7,000		
	$1,042,000		$562,000
		Net Worth	480,000
			$1,042,000

The Veeps have simple wills leaving everything to one another and upon the survivor's death to their teen-age children. The house, cars, and bank accounts are held in joint tenancy. Mr. Veep's interest in his group insurance and profit sharing plan are payable to his estate upon his death.

If Mr. Veep were to die today, a number of problems could arise in his estate. Some of these problems are as follows:

1. The HUGE stock, group life insurance, and profit sharing benefits would all be subject to probate, thereby subjecting the estate to approximately $20,000 of unnecessary executor's and attorneys' fees.
2. The Veeps' wills are not designed to minimize taxes over both deaths. As their plan now stands, the federal and state taxes on Mr. Veep's death would be $60,000 and upon Mrs. Veep's subsequent death $160,000. A proper plan can save a substantial amount of these taxes.
3. The stock loan will have to be paid off. This might force a sale of the stock at a point when the market is seriously depressed or, depending on the purchase price, force the estate to pay capital gains taxes on the stock sold.
4. Mr. Veep's $60,000 salary would cease, but the family's income needs would continue. The balance of HUGE stock left after payment of the loan and possible capital gains taxes would produce approximately $6,700 per year. The insurance and profit sharing benefits left after payment of taxes and probate costs would be approximately $100,000. Invested at 7%, this would generate another $7,000 of income. Mrs. Veep would receive approximately $9,000 from social security for a few years until the children are twenty-two. The total income is a respectable $23,700; however, $18,000 of that would be needed to continue payments on the house. Another problem which needs to be considered in connection with family income is the substantial portion which comes from the HUGE stock. If the company reduces its dividends, the effect on Mrs. Veep could be disastrous.
5. If both Mr. and Mrs. Veep were to pass away in the

near future, the children would be confronted with some serious problems. First, the wills do not nominate guardians; consequently the children may be raised by a relative with values entirely different from those of the Veep family. Also, in their state a minor becomes an adult at age eighteen. This means the children would each receive a quarter of a million dollars at a time when they might not be mature enough to handle it.

These are by no means all of the problems which might confront the Veep family in the event of Typical's death; however, they are illustrative of the situation in which many executives find themselves.

Now, let's talk about some of the things the Veeps can do to solve their problems:

1. The group life insurance and profit sharing benefits could be paid to either Mrs. Veep or a trust. In either case, the proceeds would not be subject to probate. There are two alternatives available concerning the stock; however, both have disadvantages and should not be used unless they are coordinated into the total estate plan. First, the stock could be registered in joint tenancy. This would avoid probate, but some gift taxes might be incurred and the stock could be subjected to double taxation. Second, it could be placed in a living trust. This approach would incur some current legal expenses and either annual accounting costs or trustee's fees during Mr. Veep's lifetime.
2. Several steps can be taken to reduce taxes over both deaths. First, a marital deduction trust can be drawn. Either a living trust or testamentary trust could accomplish the objective of tax reduction. Ownership of the insurance could be transferred either to the wife or to an irrevocable trust. If transferred to the wife, it will avoid taxes on the first death but increase taxes on the

second. If transferred to an irrevocable trust, all control over the policy is lost but the proceeds can avoid taxation altogether if the trust is properly designed.

3. The stock loan presents a more difficult problem. While the 5% company loan might have to be paid off, it is possible the heirs could borrow enough from their bank, pledging the stock as collateral to avoid a forced sale. The new loan would have to be repaid at some point and it would probably be at a considerably higher rate of interest. If the Veeps want to keep the stock indefinitely or avoid having it encumbered, Mr. Veep should probably acquire a sufficient amount of term insurance to cover the indebtedness. As a practical matter, the stock should probably be sold and reinvested to provide both diversification and a higher yield. The choice is up to Mr. Veep. He can make a decision today and provide the means to implement that decision or allow his personal representative or trustee to make the decision after his death.
4. Income replacement is also a difficult problem. If Mr. Veep is insurable and can afford a substantial amount of life insurance, this can provide a solution. Mr. Veep's company might be willing to install a split-dollar life insurance plan which would enable him to obtain a large amount of insurance for a relatively low expenditure. Sale of the stock and reinvestment of the proceeds can also help. For example, if the sale nets $300,000 and the proceeds are invested at 7%, it will generate $21,000 of income—three times what the dividends would provide.
5. Even if the Veeps do not commence their comprehensive estate planning at this time, they should have their attorney prepare new wills in which they name the people who should raise their children in the event both of them should pass away. Those wills should also establish a trust which would guarantee

that the children's needs and education are provided for, but withhold distribution of substantial amounts of money until they are mature enough to handle it.

Many major corporations encourage their executives to plan their estates. Some provide comprehensive financial planning assistance as a fringe benefit at substantial cost to the company. Others offer to pay attorney fees involved in planning the estate. Some corporations offer what is called the "cafeteria" approach to fringe benefits, allowing their executives to select those things which are most needed in implementing their estate plans.

The corporate executive who plans to stay with his company until retirement can utilize his fringe benefits to great advantage. On the other hand, if he is constantly looking for better opportunities, he should attempt to make his estate plan stand independent of those benefits.

CONCLUSION

Most of the average corporate executive's estate is comprised of fringe-benefit-type assets. The coordination of those assets with personal assets is the most difficult task facing the estate planner because corporate benefits are subject to change at the whim of the company and cannot always be depended upon.

CHAPTER XXIII

ESTATE PLANNING FOR FARMERS

Farmers and ranchers are among the more difficult businessmen to plan for. Their inherent independence and natural distrust of city dwellers makes it virtually impossible for an urbanized tax expert to gain their confidence. They will often go to a local attorney with limited expertise in estate planning who is equally unwilling to associate with a specialist from a big city law firm. This has resulted in chaotic consequences in the past. Hopefully the new breed of college-educated agribusiness owners are more objective where estate planning is concerned.

An invariable goal of the farmer is to keep the farm in the family. This objective is the contributing cause toward most of the farmer's estate planning problems.

Let's take a look at a typical farmer's estate. Mr. Raisen Cane and his wife, Sugar, are fifty-five and fifty years of age respectively. They have three children, one of whom, Harry, is working with his father on the farm. The daughter is married to a doctor and lives in another state. The other son is a banker in the state capital. The original farm was relatively small but over the years Mr. Cane has acquired additional acreage and today owns 1,600 acres valued at $500 per acre. Machinery and equipment are worth about $100,000 and the residence, automobiles, and personal effects have a value of approximately $80,000. Mr. Cane has a $5,000 life insurance policy payable to Sugar and about $15,000 in a bank account. At the present time, he has an operating loan from the local bank of $100,000. Some of the assets are in Mr. Cane's name alone while others are held as joint tenants. Three years ago the farm had a net income of $60,000, two years ago $20,000, and in the latest year $80,000.

Mr. Cane has an old will drawn in 1960 which leaves everything he has to his wife and if she does not survive to the children. Mrs. Cane does not have a will. When asked for his objectives, Mr. Cane indicated he would like to have Harry continue to operate the farm to support Mrs. Cane during her lifetime. Upon Mrs. Cane's death, he would like to have the three children share equally in the proceeds from operating the farm. He definitely does not want the farm sold.

PROBLEMS

Under Mr. Cane's existing estate plan, a great many problems exist. The primary problem is *lack of liquidity.* Each time he has accumulated some cash it has been reinvested in more acreage and new and better equipment. If Mr. Cane would die today, there would be liquidity problems in two areas: operating capital and estate settlement costs. There is already a $100,000 loan outstanding and it is uncertain at this point how much additional credit the bank will extend to Sugar if she continues to operate the farm. It is probably safe to assume any loan she could obtain would have to be secured by a mortgage on the farm. Taxes, probate costs, funeral expenses, and so forth would probably be in the neighborhood of $126,700. Assuming $25,000 in probate costs and $5,000 in other expenses, Mr. Cane's federal estate tax would be calculated as follows:

Gross estate		$1,000,000
Less:		
Bank loan	$100,000	
Probate costs	25,000	
Misc. expenses	5,000	
		130,000
Adjusted gross estate		$870,000
Less marital deduction		435,000
Taxable estate		$435,000
Tax on $435,000		
Tax on $250,000		$80,800
Tax on $185,000 @ 34%		62,900
Total tax		143,700
Less unified credit		47,000
Estate tax payable		$96,700

The calculation above does not take into consideration state death taxes which could be substantial. This is offset somewhat by the fact we did not deduct the credit for state death taxes from the federal estate tax. The total liquidity need in Mr. Cane's estate would be about $226,700 if we include the bank loan. Problem number one, lack of liquidity upon Mr. Cane's death, has been clearly identified.

The second problem is the excessive tax and lack of liquidity upon Mrs. Cane's subsequent death. Assuming all of the above costs are paid, Mrs. Cane will have an estate of $773,300 ($1,000,000 – $226,700). Inasmuch as she does not have a will, let's assume her probate expenses, funeral bills, and so forth will be slightly less than Mr. Cane's—$23,300 should cover everything. Mrs. Cane's federal estate tax would be calculated as follows:

Gross estate	$773,300
Less probate expense	23,300
Taxable estate	$750,000
Tax on $750,000	$248,300
Less unified tax credit	47,000
Estate tax payable	$201,300

This estate tax would be reduced somewhat if Mrs. Cane's death follows her husband's by less than ten years; however, it would also be increased for state death taxes which are not taken into consideration in this illustration. The shrinkage in Mr. and Mrs. Cane's million-dollar estate would be $451,300, leaving the children with a net estate of $548,700. This shrinkage can be reduced with proper planning.

The third problem relates to an inequity in which their son, Harry, is concerned. He is expected to assume all of the responsibilities of managing the farm for his mother's benefit during her lifetime and then become an equal partner with his brother and sister upon Mrs. Cane's death. It is fairly easy to manipulate farm income and if Harry is the least bit envious of his brother and sister, he could plow any profits back into the farm and there would be very little that could be done about it.

The final problem is the potential capital gain tax when the property is sold. This may not be a problem for many years if the farm continues to be managed by the family, but what if part of the property has to be sold to pay taxes? Under the old law, the cost basis for capital gain tax purposes was increased to the market value at date of death. As mentioned in Chapter VI, the 1976 Tax Reform Act changed that. It provides a "fresh start" for property acquired before 1980, but the basis of property acquired after 1979 will be the decedent's cost. From our set of facts, it would be impossible to approximate a tax, but sufficient to say that some capital gain tax will be due upon sale. One stated purpose of the 1976 Tax Reform Act was to provide farmers with some relief. Unfortunately this was more political rhetoric than fact. If anything, the farmers were hurt more by the imposition of restrictive controls and the new post-death capital gain tax. As long as they can afford to own and operate their farm within the family they are protected, but the moment the family wants out of farming tax costs skyrocket.

SOLUTIONS

There are several alternatives available to us in planning a farmer's estate.

Defer Payment of Tax—First, you will recall from Chapter VI that under certain circumstances the time for payment of federal estate tax attributable to the farm itself can be extended for up to fifteen years. Mr. Cane's estate qualifies for this extension, but keep in mind, the tax still has to be paid. It is only deferred by this provision. Adequate income must be generated by the farm to provide for Harry and Mrs. Cane as well as pay the tax. Also, it is only the estate tax attributable to the farm which can be deferred. Probate costs, funeral expenses, and demand obligations will have to be paid shortly after death. If they decide to sell the farm, the estate tax immediately becomes due and payable. The same thing happens if they decide to discontinue farming. In addition, the heirs are personally liable for the tax. If the property should decrease in value due to extended drought or depression, the heirs would still be liable for the tax based on date of death values.

Life Insurance—If Mr. and Mrs. Cane can qualify, it would probably be advisable to acquire sufficient life insurance to cover their estate settlement costs and give the family a little extra cash with which to operate the farm.

Irrevocable Life Insurance Trust—They might consider placing the insurance in an irrevocable life insurance trust to avoid taxation in both Mr. and Mrs. Cane's estates. In order to get cash into the estate, the trust would have to have the right to either lend funds to the estate or buy assets from it. Since a sale would result in capital gain, and since the beneficiaries of the trust and the estate would be the same individuals, the trustee and executor would probably opt for the loan. By using the gift splitting privilege discussed on page 53, the Canes could contribute up to $18,000 to the trust each year with no gift tax consequence. This should enable them to acquire about $400,000 of permanent insurance from a reputable company. At a rate of $18,000 a year, the taxable estate could be reduced substantially over a ten-year period.

Marital Deduction Trust—In order to minimize taxes upon Mrs. Cane's death it would be advisable to either use a marital deduction trust such as that described on page 98 or leave the non-marital share outright to the children. If the children receive their interests direct, they have the right to sell or dispose of those interests in any way they see fit which might defeat the goal of keeping the farm intact. As you will see later, one way to avoid this problem would be incorporation. The costs on Mr. Cane's estate would be the same using the marital deduction trust; however, Mrs. Cane would now have an estate of $435,000 (the maximum marital deduction). Her estate would probably be subject to probate costs and funeral expenses of about $25,000. Mrs. Cane's estate tax would be calculated as follows:

Gross estate	$435,000
Less probate expense	25,000
Taxable estate	$410,000
Tax on $410,000	125,200
Less unified tax credit	47,000
Estate tax payable	$ 78,200

Mrs. Cane's estate settlement costs would be $103,200, the costs over both deaths $319,900, and the amount distributable to the children $670,100. The marital deduction trust would save the estate $121,400.

Valuation—Chapter VII illustrates some of the valuation problems confronting a farmer's estate. For our purposes, we will assume Mr. Cane's land is currently being put to its highest and best use. Any other assumption would result in higher probate expenses due to the executors' more expanded duties. In any event, this is not a planning decision that has to be made prior to death. If the personal representative and the heirs decide a different value would be advisable, that can be determined after death. For planning purposes, we should always assume the property will be valued at its highest and best use.

Gifts to the Children—Prior to the 1976 Tax Reform Act it was possible to transfer substantial amounts of property to the children at relatively low rates. Today, there is very little advantage to making gifts other than the fact that $3,000 per year, per person, is excluded in calculating the tax and the appreciation on property transferred will inure to the donee. Farmers in high income tax brackets might want to transfer interests in the farm in order to shift part of the income into lower tax brackets. This will be discussed further in relation to incorporation or partnership.

Family Partnership—Mr. Cane might consider forming a limited partnership with himself as the general partner and his wife and children as limited partners. A limited partnership is one in which the limited partners' liability extends only to their contributed capital. The general partner assumes all other liability and manages the partnership. If a limited partner becomes involved in management or allows his name to be used in the company name, he will be treated as a general partner. When Mr. Cane dies, his son, Harry, could be substituted as the general partner. The limited partnership enables income to be shifted to the limited partners. Mr. Cane would receive a management salary and excess income distributed among the limited partners. Mr. and Mrs. Cane could transfer interests in the partnership to the children and grandchildren at the rate of $6,000 per person, per year, with no adverse tax consequences. If there are three children and six grandchildren, the Canes could transfer $54,000 in partnership interests each year with no federal gift tax.

Quite often both spouses have made substantial contributions to the success of the farm. The wife may be responsible for egg production, milking, record keeping, banking, and so forth. She might also help with planting and harvesting which would be valid contributions. On the other hand, her domestic services such as cooking, cleaning, and laundering would probably not be considered. If assets are held in joint tenancy, that joint tenancy might be treated as an unwritten partnership in which each spouse has an interest. If it is possible to imply a partnership from the facts, a formal partnership agreement can be written which reduces the couple's understanding to writing. The advantage of this approach is that each spouse would be treated as owning one-half of the estate and taxes would be reduced upon the first death. For example, instead of a $1,000,000 estate, Mr. Cane would be considered as having an estate of $500,000. If he takes advantage of the maximum marital deduction, taxes on his death would be calculated as follows:

Gross estate		$500,000
Less bank loan	$50,000	
Probate costs	20,000	
Misc. expense	5,000	
		75,000
Adjusted gross estate		425,000
Marital deduction		250,000
Taxable estate		175,000
Tax on $175,000		46,800
Less credit		47,000
Tax payable		-0-

As you can see, the tax savings on the first death would be $86,700; however, on Mrs. Cane's subsequent death taxes would be increased from $201,300 to $236,400. The overall savings would be $51,600.

Gross estate	$875,000
Probate costs, etc.	35,000
Taxable estate	840,000

(*Continued*)

Tax on $840,000	283,400
Less credit	47,000
	$236,400

Incorporation—Incorporation could also facilitate the transfer of ownership and assure the farm staying in the family. Very few farms are presently incorporated. Some states either prohibit or restrict farmers from incorporating. North Dakota, for example, prohibits farms from incorporating whereas Kansas only permits incorporation if the corporation has ten or less stockholders and consists of no more than 5,000 acres. Transfers of ownership can be effected by simple stock certificates rather than executing deeds each time gifts are made. Corporations cost more. The mechanics of operation, record keeping, maintaining minutes, additional tax returns, and corporate social security taxes all tend to increase the cost. Unless the corporation qualifies for taxation as a partnership, and the stockholders so elect, there is likely to be double taxation of income. Most farmers have fairly substantial debts due to operating loans and mortgages. If these debts are assumed by the corporation, there will be taxable gain to the farmer to the extent those liabilities exceed his basis.

> **Example:** Bull Driver paid $100,000 for his farm in 1950. Over the years it has increased in value to $500,000. He has found it necessary to borrow periodically for operating purposes and currently has an outstanding operating loan of $150,000. If he incorporates, he will realize a capital gain of $50,000 ($150,000 liability less $100,000 basis equals $50,000 capital gain).

Part of the gain might be treated as ordinary income instead of long-term capital gain depending on the nature of the assets placed in the corporation.

Another potential problem exists where the shareholders elect to be taxed as a partnership under subchapter "S" of the Internal Revenue Code. If the liabilities exceed the basis, the taxpayers will not be allowed to deduct losses passed through the corporation. Under subchapter "S," losses are precluded when the stock has a zero basis. Real property transferred to a corporation results in a possible problem on death. Both the stock and the underlying real property will increase in value proportionately. There is a possibility that two capital gain taxes would be incurred on the same property if the land is sold first and the corporate stock second. This potential problem could be resolved through a liquidation; however, the stockholders will realize ordinary income to the extent of any accumulated earnings and profits. Since the accrual basis is usually used to calculate earnings, certain zero basis assets such as unharvested crops would be treated as earnings for this purpose. While there are many shortcomings to agri-corporations, there are also some distinct advantages. The corporation might be able to provide certain benefits like group insurance, pension plans, and medical reimbursement plans to stockholder employees with pre-tax dollars.

Private Annuity—The private annuity should be considered in most farm situations; however the instability of income would pose problems for the payor. Chapter XVII describes the advantages and disadvantages of private annuities in some detail.

CONCLUSION

The biggest problem in planning for farmers and ranchers is lack of liquidity. This fact, combined with an almost universal goal to keep the property in the family, points toward only one practical solution: life insurance. The most elaborate estate plan in the world will be ineffective if there is no cash available to pay estate settlement costs.

CHAPTER XXIV

ESTATE PLANNING FOR THE SINGLE PERSON

Single individuals are concerned with many of the same estate planning problems which bother married couples. They are willing to sacrifice, if necessary, to provide for parents, brothers, sisters, close friends, and so forth. So much of their income goes for taxes during their lifetimes, they are willing to do almost anything to avoid taxes upon their deaths. A look at a few hypothetical case studies will help to clarify some of the problems and solutions facing single individuals.

THE SYMPATHETIC SISTER

Winnie Widow and Sally Spinster are sisters in their seventies. Winnie's husband passed away two years ago after a prolonged illness. Unfortunately, that illness consumed most of their savings and Winnie was left almost entirely dependent on social security. Sally, on the other hand, had remained single. She worked for over fifty years and saved almost $200,000.

Winnie is currently living with Sally, who has more than enough for them to live comfortably. They don't have any serious financial problems today; however, Sally is concerned as to what might happen to Winnie if she should pass away. Sally has five other brothers and sisters and a dozen nieces and nephews, none of whom is well-to-do; consequently she does not want to leave her entire estate to Winnie.

Sally's attorney suggests she create a trust in her will providing that her trustee pay income or principal to whichever of her brothers and sisters is in need of help, with Winnie to be given preference. Winnie could also be given the right to live in Sally's home as long as she lives, but when she dies or moves to a retirement home, the house would be sold and the proceeds added to the trust. Upon the death of the last survivor of her brothers and sisters, the trust will terminate and be divided equally among her nieces and nephews.

Sally likes the idea, but would like to give something to her nieces and nephews immediately upon her death. Her attorney advises her to limit the outright gifts to $1,000 each in order to make certain there will be enough money left to protect Winnie and the other brothers and sisters. When the will is completed, Sally will have done everything she can to assure her family will be provided for.

THE BENEVOLENT BACHELOR

Ted Teacher, age sixty, is an economics professor at I.O.U. A confirmed bachelor, he has devoted his life to the study of stock-market trends. Much of his considerable wealth has been amassed by applying the theory of astrotiming, a concept which he developed utilizing the relationship between astrology and stock-market trends.

Most of Ted's associates scoff at his theory in spite of the fact it has worked for him. Ted is in poor health and he is concerned he will not be able to scientifically prove his theory during his lifetime. He would like his estate to be used for the research necessary to prove or disprove the concept; however, he is concerned that if he leaves his money to the university itself, his colleagues will find other uses for the funds.

Ted's attorney, E. S. Tate, suggests that Ted create a trust from which the income can be paid to I.O.U. each year to support the necessary research. The trustees would be required to approve the research budget and review the results annually. Once the theory is proved or disproved to their satisfaction, income will be used to provide scholarships in the field of economics.

Mr. Tate believes such a trust would qualify as a charitable gift and suggests that if Ted would create the trust now and place some of his assets in it each year during his lifetime, he might realize some significant income-tax savings.

By placing $50,000 per year in such a trust and retaining the right to receive an annual income of 6%, Ted might qualify for a $17,000 income tax deduction. Upon Ted's death, his will could pour the balance of his estate into the existing trust. Ted likes the plan because it not only guarantees that his research desires will be fulfilled but also will provide him with more spendable income during his lifetime.

THE DUTIFUL DAUGHTER

Mary Martyr, age thirty-seven, has assumed the responsibility for her widowed, invalid mother. Mary, a legal secretary, earns $15,000 per year. She and her mother live in a small apartment and have accumulated very little except for $10,000 in a savings account. Mary also has a $10,000 life insurance policy where she works.

Mary is concerned about what would happen to her mother if she (Mary) were to pass away prematurely. The only income available to Mrs. Martyr, other than her social security, would be interest from the savings account and insurance proceeds remaining after paying estate settlement costs. Without additional income Mrs. Martyr could possibly become dependent on welfare.

Mary asked her boss to help her find a solution to her problem. He suggested that, since she had exhibited the ability to save, she consider using life insurance in her savings program. If she passes away, the proceeds would generate enough income to make her mother independent. If she lives to retirement, the cash values can be used to supplement her retirement income.

An insurance man in whom her boss had confidence illustrated how much income could be created if Mary would invest $100 per month. He used a participating ordinary life policy with dividends accumulating at interest and came up with the following: In the event of Mary's death, there would be $75,000 of insurance proceeds which would produce $550 per month for her mother's lifetime. If Mary should live to age sixty-five, the cash values and accumulated dividends would total about $60,000. This cash could be withdrawn and invested or taken in installments. If taken under a non-refund annuity, approximately $440 per month would be available to supplement her retirement income.

THE ODD COUPLE

René, age fifty, and Michel, age forty-five, have been close friends for years. René has an extremely successful decorating business and Michel teaches at the university. They live together in René's posh Beverly Hills condominium with René's mother, age seventy-five, who is the only member of either family to have accepted their relationship.

A few weeks ago René was diagnosed to have cancer and immediately contacted a well-known estate planning attorney. René wants to make certain that both mother and Michel are well taken care of for their lifetimes but does not want any other family members to receive anything.

The estate was estimated at $1,000,000. René's attorney indicated that if the estate were left equally to Michel and René's mother, the federal estate and California inheritance taxes would total $412,000. René was flabbergasted. The remaining assets would not be enough to enable mother and Michel to maintain their standard of living.

The attorney advised René the only way other family members could be precluded from participating in the estate would be to create a trust and that the trust could be designed to substantially reduce taxes. Due to the uniqueness of the situation, he told René it might take several weeks to come up with the best solution.

About three weeks later, the attorney called René with a plan that would save $230,000 in taxes and estate settlement costs.

First of all, it was decided to place most of the assets in a living trust in order to minimize estate settlement costs. A part of the estate was subjected to probate in order to create an additional taxable entity and minimize over-all income taxes as well as make certain any creditors would be limited to four months in which to present their claims.

Upon René's death, the trust divides into two separate charitable remainder unitrusts from which mother and Michel would each receive about $23,000 per year, and the remainder after their deaths would go to the American Cancer Society. The trusts were not equal at the outset because under California law blood relations are taxed at lower rates than unrelated parties; consequently the tax on Michel's share is greater than the tax on the mother's share. In addition, the deductible portion of the trust for a seventy-five-year-old is far greater than for a forty-five-year-old. As a result the actual division was arrived at through application of a very complicated formula.

René was pleased with the plan. It provided the maximum possible income for mother and Michel. It precluded any other person from receiving any part of the estate and it minimized the portion of the estate confiscated by the state and federal government; and, ultimately, the estate would be used to help find a cure for cancer.

René died with peace of mind.

THE ANTICIPATING AUNT

Aunt Teak, who turned eighty last year, has a houseful of treasures acquired by her family over several lifetimes. She is loved and respected by her many nieces and nephews, who visit her often. Whenever one of them admires a particular item, Aunt Teak makes a note of it so that she can give it to that person in her will. Aunt Teak realizes how impractical it is to change her will every time she decides to give a specific item to a specific niece or nephew; however, she also understands people; consequently, if she is not specific, there may be bickering among the family when she passes away.

Aunt Teak met with her attorney to discuss the problem and he advised her the solution was quite simple. Their state, and many others, had recently enacted a law which enables her to maintain a list independent from her will indicating which items she wants to go to each heir. That list can be changed as often as she wants without the necessity for changing her will.

He also reminded her that at her age she is susceptible to physical or mental infirmity, and to protect herself and her loved ones she should consider either a living trust or conservatorship to protect her substantial assets. Their local bank has an excellent trust department which would be happy to help her whichever approach she decides to take. They decided on the living trust because she wants to continue directing investments as long as she is mentally capable and would be unable to do so under the conservatorship.

One other suggestion the attorney made, which is wise advice for all of us, is for Aunt Teak to make a complete inventory of every item in her house and have an antique appraiser value her collection. This appraisal will help her insurance man to provide proper coverage. While the items themselves are irreplaceable, there is no reason to lose their economic value if they are stolen or destroyed. In addition, it will be a handy reference for Aunt Teak when deciding what items should go to which individual and a checklist for her executor to make certain no items are removed from the house by an overzealous heir.

Aunt Teak followed all of her attorney's suggestions and is now comfortable in knowing she has done everything in her power to protect herself during her lifetime and give her heirs what she thinks they will enjoy and appreciate after her death.

CONCLUSION

The foregoing illustrations presented just a few of the estate planning problems which confront single people. Even what appears to be a relatively simple situation requires some planning. Competent trust officers, attorneys, and some life insurance men can help to identify these problems and suggest possible solutions.

CHAPTER XXV

PLANNING TO PROTECT THE HANDICAPPED PERSON

Physical and mental handicaps are more prevalent than most people realize. The President's Committee on Employment of the Handicapped in 1971 estimated there were eighteen million physically handicapped adults and twenty million with severe mental disorders. Some of these people were born with their disabilities and others acquired them at some time during their lives. Some have the ability to earn a reasonable living, many are severely restricted as to the types of jobs they can handle, and others are unemployable. The purpose of this chapter is to describe ways in which relatives of handicapped persons can provide for their continued well-being. Each person's problems and abilities are somewhat different, but there are certain suggestions applicable to most situations. In order to relate our suggestions to specific situations, several case studies are included. These case studies help to illustrate most of the planning alternatives available to you.

Most handicapped people who work (particularly the mentally retarded) receive below-average incomes. Those who are unable to work are dependent upon various state and federal programs for their support. In either case, they will probably require supplemental income to live comfortably.

Physically handicapped individuals are as capable of handling their financial affairs as anyone; however, their disabilities often make them dependent upon others for many of their personal needs. There are a great many unscrupulous people in this world who will not hesitate to take advantage of a handicapped person. I have observed many examples of practical nurses and companions who have gained the love and confidence of disabled individuals and then taken advantage of them financially. Because of the possibility of this problem, the handicapped may need professional assistance in handling their financial affairs.

Mentally retarded individuals should never be burdened with the management of large amounts of money. Investment decisions require abilities that even the slightly retarded may not possess. In virtually every situation the retarded person should have assistance in managing financial affairs.

Parents of handicapped children are equally, or more, concerned about who will watch out for the child's well-being as they are about how well he is provided for financially. In most states the parents can nominate a guardian for the child in their wills and that nomination will usually be honored by the court. Most guardianships terminate when a child becomes an adult; however, if the child is developmentally disabled, there is often provision for the guardianship to continue. Quite often a brother, sister, aunt, or uncle will be willing to assume this responsibility. If there are no relatives who are capable or willing, the parents may want to ask for suggestions from one of the local associations which provide services for handicapped individuals.

It is important for your attorney, the guardian, and your trustee (if a trust is used) to understand your desires and those of the child concerning such things as his education, the possible need for institutionalization, and his ability to adjust to society. It would be extremely helpful to all parties if you would write a letter of instructions reflecting your desires and detailing the actions you believe would be in your child's best interests.

Those parents who are fortunate enough to have sufficient assets to provide for their handicapped child after their deaths must make a determination as to how those assets will be distributed. If they go outright to a retarded child, a conservator would probably be appointed by the court to manage his assets for him. This is usually a costly and inflexible procedure. In addition, the child may be precluded from receiving any form of government assistance. If he is eligible for government assistance, the agency providing support will have a claim against his assets. A slightly retarded child who is independent and receives assets outright might be taken advantage of because of his gullibility.

The most practical way to provide for a handicapped child is to create a trust. A trust is more flexible than a conservatorship and less costly. There are a number of advantages which cannot be obtained in any other way. In smaller estates where there are several children, the trust can be held as a single fund and the trustee given broad discretion to use funds for any of the children. In effect, he would try to disburse funds as you would if you were still alive. This is where the letter of instructions mentioned earlier is particularly valuable. Upon the handicapped child's death, the balance of the trust could be distributed to his brothers and sisters.

In larger estates, a separate trust might be established for the handicapped child. Upon his death, that trust could be distributed either to the surviving brothers and sisters or perhaps to an organization which provides research into the causes and cures of his disability or which provides services to the handicapped. As you can see, the alternatives are virtually unlimited.

You can impose certain specific duties upon the trustee or the guardian relating to the child's care. Periodic inspections of the child's living conditions and the treatment he is receiving can be required in the trust document. That individual should also make certain the child is obtaining available specialized training and education.

It is important for your child to know he has a friend who will visit him periodically and make certain he is not being taken advantage of. Whoever this individual is he should be reasonably compensated for his time and expenses. Many people do not have friends or relatives to whom they would entrust this responsibility. Hopefully, state associations will eventually have adequate funds to hire professional "friends" for handicapped individuals.

A trust provides a way of assuring proper management of assets and guaranteeing that someone will be attempting to make those assets last for the child's lifetime. Where the estate is large enough, it would be advisable to employ a corporate trustee who could work closely with the guardian or some other advisor who understands the problems of the handicapped. The executive director of your association or another parent who has been active with the association could make excellent advisors to the corporate trustee.

You should check with corporate fiduciaries in your area to determine the minimum-size estate they would be willing to handle. In many larger cities banks and trust companies will not accept accounts under $100,000, and if they do their fees may be prohibitive.

If it is impractical to name a corporate trustee due to the size of your estate, a family member or friend might be willing to serve. Restricting investments to savings accounts, certificates of deposit, and treasury bonds will make his job easier as will the letter of instructions which will help him in making distributions.

Many handicapped children are institutionalized. Under no circumstances should your assets be left directly to that institution while your child is alive. It can go bankrupt, the quality of care might deteriorate, or any number of other things might happen to make it undesirable for your child. Once the money has been given to the institution, it cannot be retrieved. If you are sincerely interested in providing for the institution itself, leave the money in trust during your child's lifetime and distribute it to the institution after his death.

The trust which you create for your child's support must be carefully drafted by a knowledgeable attorney. The state or a public institution, under most state laws, can obtain reimbursement from any funds available to the child. If the trust specifically provides that it is intended to furnish benefits supplemental to public support, it is likely any claim for reimbursement will be disallowed.

CASE STUDY I

Mr. and Mrs. Capp have three children. Their oldest child, Bill, is slightly retarded. He attends a special school and it is likely he will be able to partially support himself. The other two children are considered normal. The Capps are by no means wealthy. While they are alive, they can help Bill a little, but with two other children to raise and educate that help will be modest for several years. Mr. Capp is concerned about how the family will be provided for in the event of his death, but he is even more concerned about what would happen to them if both he and Mrs. Capp should pass away. Their financial statement would look as follows:

ASSETS		*LIABILITIES*	
Residence	$50,000	Mortgage	$30,000
Cash in bank	3,000	Auto loan	1,500
Automobile	3,000	Boat loan	5,000
Personal effects	10,000	Camper loan	1,500
Camper and boat	10,000	Misc. debts	1,000
	$76,000		$39,000
Net worth			$37,000

In addition Mr. Capp has $20,000 of group insurance and another $20,000 of personal insurance. He earns about $18,000 a year.

Mr. Capp's insurance man agreed to help them analyze their situation and determine what steps could be taken to protect the family. It was decided if Mr. Capp passed away first the camper and boat would be sold to pay off all debts except the mortgage. Thirty thousand dollars of the existing insurance would be used to pay off the mortgage. This would leave the family with a cash reserve of about $10,000 after last illness and funeral expenses. Mrs. Capp would receive about $700 a month in social security income; however, this would be reduced as each child attains age eighteen. Bill would receive benefits until he is twenty-two years old if he is in school; however, he might not be able to go to school because of the limited funds available. Bill qualifies for $167 per month from a special government program after he attains age eighteen, but if he is able to earn even a modest living that government support will terminate. Once the children are raised, Mrs. Capp will probably have to go to work. She is untrained; consequently any job she obtains will probably be menial.

Mr. Capp was appalled at the situation. He wouldn't want his wife to be forced to go to work. He would like to help the normal children obtain a college education if they have the capability and he wants to help Bill become an independent, self-sufficient adult. What can he do?

The insurance man suggested a two-step approach. First, he would need to generate more income for the family through additional life insurance, and second, a trust would have to be drawn by a knowledgeable attorney who understands how to best provide for family members with varying needs. Mr. Capp is concerned about the cost of both the insurance and the attorney's fees. The insurance man suggests he obtain $100,000 of the cheapest term insurance available with the idea they can convert part of it to permanent insurance as his circumstances improve. He also convinces Mr. Capp an investment in attorney fees today will return peace of mind tomorrow.

Several days later they meet with the attorney who suggests a life insurance trust which will provide for Mrs. Capp during her lifetime and allow her a great deal of flexibility in using funds to provide for the children's education and to help support Bill. The corporate trustee would be available to counsel with her so that she would not deplete the trust to her own detriment. Upon Mrs. Capp's death, the trustee is able to use the funds to provide for each child who happens to be in need. It is anticipated that Bill might have the greatest need; consequently the trust will continue for his lifetime. Ad Vocate, the local director of the Association of Retarded Citizens, or his successor, is appointed as an advisor to the trustee concerning Bill's needs. Upon Bill's death, if the other two children are over twenty-five, any remaining balance in the trust will be distributed to them.

Mr. and Mrs. Capp now have the peace of mind their insurance man told them they would have and they agree the investment in both the insurance and the attorney fees were wise investments on their part.

CASE STUDY II

Mr. and Mrs. Rich have four children. The youngest child, Vera, was seriously injured when she fell off her horse a few years ago and is a paraplegic. She is an intelligent girl who plans to become a CPA. While she is fairly self-sufficient, she will probably need a part-time companion-housekeeper in the future. The other three children are presently in college and doing fairly well.

Mr. Rich is a successful contractor who has amassed an estate of $800,000; however, he has given very little thought to estate planning. Mrs. Rich has been encouraging him to get a will but he is always too busy.

One day he learned that a former employee who had received a $100,000 settlement as a result of an industrial accident had been bilked out of his money by a girl who had pretended to be in love with him. He had transferred the money into a joint bank account with her and within a few days she had withdrawn every penny.

Recognizing how susceptible handicapped people can be to the attention and apparent affection of others, Mr. Rich decided to do something to protect his daughter from a similar situation. Needless to say, Mrs. Rich was relieved that he had finally decided to take action.

His attorney recommended a marital deduction trust to take effect upon his death to minimize taxes and provide management for Mrs. Rich. Upon Mrs. Rich's death, the trust would divide into four equal parts, one for each child. The three healthy children would receive distributions as they gain maturity, but Vera's share would remain in trust for her lifetime. She is unable to have children; consequently upon her death the trust would be divided among her brothers and sisters.

Inasmuch as Mr. Rich is in a very high income tax bracket, the attorney suggested he might want to place some income-producing assets into an irrevocable trust for Vera's benefit to give her a feeling of independence. Mr. Rich liked the idea, but he felt he should treat the children equally; consequently he placed $50,000 in trust for each child thereby shifting $12,000 of income from his 70% tax bracket to their very low brackets. The after tax savings to the Rich family amounted to over $5,000 per year.

Mr. Rich is excited about his estate plan and pleased at the way Vera is being provided for.

CASE STUDY III

Ms. Devor See has one child, Summer, who is severely retarded. Summer lives at home and would be unable to take care of herself if Ms. See were to pass away. Ms. See owns a small business and is moderately successful. If she were to pass away, her estate would probably exceed $100,000. If Ms. See passes away Summer will probably be sent to an institution. There is a slight possibility she could live in a special residence for the developmentally disabled, but it is too early to consider that possibility.

Ms. See wants to be certain Summer is well taken care of during her lifetime but would like the assets to be used for research in the area of retardation after Summer's death. Her attorney suggests a trust be created which authorizes the trustee to supplement Summer's support from public sources. The income generated from Ms. See's assets would be more than adequate to provide that supplemental support, and the assets themselves would be kept intact to provide for important research. Ms. See nominates her sister as Summer's guardian. The sister has always exhibited sincere interest in Summer's well-being and has become an active board member of the Association of Retarded Citizens.

Ms. See now knows she has done everything in her power to protect Summer and provide for her well-being. She also knows her assets will ultimately be used to help other retarded children to maximize their potential.

CONCLUSION

Planning for the protection of handicapped individuals requires more than guaranteeing funds for their support. It requires an understanding of each person's disability and his potential for independence. The planner must know what benefits are available through public and private organizations and what steps need to be taken to obtain those benefits. A competent and compassionate advocate (guardian or advisor) needs to be selected to watch out for the handicapped person's best interests. If there is more than one child in the family, each child's needs must be taken into consideration.

In most instances, a trust will be the ideal vehicle to provide for the handicapped child. Where possible the trustee should be a bank or trust company experienced in managing other people's money. The child's advocate should work closely with the trustee in making certain the child receives everything he needs to be comfortable. Upon the child's death, the trustee can make distribution to surviving children or to whomever the settlor directs.

INDEX